D0616976

The Reckless Mind
Intellectuals in Politics

The Reckless Mind
Intellectuals in Politics

Mark Lilla

NEW YORK REVIEW BOOKS

New York

THIS IS A NEW YORK REVIEW BOOK
PUBLISHED BY THE NEW YORK REVIEW OF BOOKS

THE RECKLESS MIND:
INTELLECTUALS IN POLITICS
by Mark Lilla

Copyright © 2001 by NYREV, Inc.

All rights reserved.

This edition published in 2001
in the United States of America by
The New York Review of Books
1755 Broadway
New York, NY 10019
www.nybooks.com

HM728
.L55
2001

046640589

Library of Congress Cataloging-in-Publication Data
Lilla, Mark.
    The reckless mind : intellectuals in politics / by Mark Lilla.
      p. cm.
    ISBN 0-940322-76-5 (hardcover : alk. paper)
    1. Intellectuals — Europe — History — 20th century. 2. Europe —
Intellectual life — 20th century. 3. Totalitarianism — History —
20th century. I. Title.
    HM728 .L55 2001
    305.5'52'094 — dc21

                                                        2001001857

ISBN 0-940322-76-5

Printed in the United States of America on acid-free paper.

September 2001

Third Printing

For Daniel Bell

Contents

PREFACE

J'aimerais mieux la lecture des vies particulières
pour commencer l'étude du cœur humain.
—Rousseau

Each life converges to some center.
—Emily Dickinson

IN 1953 THE Polish poet Czesław Miłosz, then unknown
in the West, published *The Captive Mind*, a study of
how intellectuals in postwar Poland were conforming to
the Stalinist orthodoxies of dialectical materialism and
socialist realism. The cold war was at its peak when the
book appeared, earning it much attention and translation into several languages. Yet *The Captive Mind* was
no mere cold war pamphlet. It remains a moving and
disturbing book to this day, not least because Miłosz
chose to dwell on ordinary cases rather than the most
extreme ones. Writers who suffered physical intimida-
tion or prison do not appear in his pages, nor do the

x

commissars and satraps who hounded them. Miłosz instead sketched portraits of four rather successful writers, describing in detail their intellectual and political wanderings in pre-war Poland (usually on the nationalist and anti-Semitic right), their war experiences (often heroic), and their adjustment to the Communist regime imposed by the Soviet Union. In each case Miłosz fixed upon an aspect of the writer's character that revealed itself early on in life and showed how it shaped his later writing and shifting political engagements. We meet Alpha, "the moralist"; Beta, the nihilist whose "nihilism results from an ethical passion, from disappointed love of the world"; Gamma, "the slave of history"; and finally the poet Delta, "the troubadour." The sketches can be read as documents of a dark historical moment, but what makes them memorable is their insight into the depths of human psychology. Miłosz did not moralize, nor did he present himself as omniscient about the course of history. (After the war he too had seen hope for his country in communism and served the Polish government as cultural attaché in Washington and Paris until 1951, when he sought asylum in the West.) His aim was to show, by example, what happens when certain characters, certain kinds of minds, are thrust into the whirlwind of politics.

Miłosz's sketches are humbling. But they are also puzzling. History dealt a bad hand to thinkers and writers who lived behind the Iron Curtain; some played it well, resisting the tyrant's bribes and threats as best they could, others joined the chorus. Those of us who have never faced such choices are poorly placed to judge what they did. But how are we to explain the fact that a chorus for tyranny also existed in countries where intellectuals faced no danger and were free to write as they pleased? What possibly could have induced *them* to justify the actions of modern tyrants or, as was more common, to deny any essential difference between tyranny and the free societies of the West? Fascist and Communist regimes were welcomed with open arms by many West European intellectuals throughout the twentieth century, as were countless "national liberation" movements that instantly became traditional tyrannies, bringing misery to unfortunate peoples across the globe. Throughout the century Western liberal democracy was portrayed in diabolical terms as the real home of tyranny —the tyranny of capital, of imperialism, of bourgeois conformity, of "metaphysics," of "power," even of "language." The facts were rarely in dispute; they were apparent to anyone who read the newspapers and had a sense of moral proportion. No, something deeper was at work in the minds of these European intellectuals, something reckless. How do such minds operate? we wonder. And what are they seeking in politics?

This book attempts to address these questions and can be read as a modest companion to *The Captive Mind*. It is not a systematic treatise, since what it has to say can best be learned by studying intellectual and political lives in concrete historical situations. A great deal was written in the last century about "intellectual responsibility," a senseless term, and about the question whether a thinker's thought can be separated from the political uses to which he puts it. This has always seemed to me *une question mal posée*. At one level, the answer must be "yes": the truth of Euclid's proofs is not affected by how he may have treated his servants. But grownups know that serious thinkers writing about serious matters are not engaged in geometric parlor games; they are writing out of the deepest wells of their experiences as they try to orient themselves in the world. Their works and their activities, including their political activities, are traces left by this quest. If we are on similar journeys, we owe it to ourselves to reflect upon what they did and why.

Any number of twentieth-century European thinkers might have been selected as subjects for philosophical-political profiles. I have chosen to focus on some whose thought is still alive for us in this century, in the hope that readers will come away convinced that the problems addressed here did not evaporate in 1989. The fact that so many admirers of these thinkers continue to ignore or justify their political recklessness was an added consideration. I have chosen thinkers on both sides of the Rhine, and on both the ideological left and right, to show that the phenomenon they represent is not limited to one nation or political tendency. As for the lessons one might draw from these sketches, they are examined in the afterword, which readers are encouraged to consider after touring this gallery.

A final word on the thinkers discussed here. It is not my intention in these critical profiles to offer readers an excuse for dismissing these figures as somehow beyond the pale of decency. Quite the contrary: I myself have been drawn to them and over the years have learned from their works. But as I learned from them, my sense of disappointment only grew, a disappointment I found best expressed in a short notebook entry made by Karl Jaspers à propos of Martin Heidegger and other German thinkers who welcomed the arrival of tyranny in 1933. His sentiment is my own.

xiii

> Despite my distance from them I feel affection for these men—different kinds of affection since they are so different from each other. But this affection never develops into love. It's as if I want to implore them to place the loftiness of their minds in the service of better powers. Greatness of mind becomes an object of love only when the power at work in it itself has a noble character.

MARK LILLA

Chapter I

MARTIN HEIDEGGER

HANNAH ARENDT

KARL JASPERS

WHAT HAS PHILOSOPHY to do with love? If Plato is to be believed, everything. While all lovers are not philosophers, philosophers are the only true lovers, since they alone understand what love blindly seeks. Love evokes in us all an unconscious memory of the beauty of the Ideas, and this memory maddens us; we feel possessed by a frenzied yearning to couple and to "beget in the beautiful," as the *Symposium* beautifully puts it (209b). Those who possess self-control mate intellectually and commune with the Ideas, which is philosophy's aim, while those who lack it purge their passions in the flesh and remain bound to the world.

It is because erotic desire does not always issue in philosophy that it must be treated with utmost care, Plato teaches. When eros is unleashed in an immoderate person the soul sinks into sensual pleasure, love of money, drunkenness, even madness. So strong is its power that eros can overwhelm our reason and natural instincts, directing them to its own ends and becoming the soul's tyrant. What is political tyranny, Plato has Socrates ask in the *Republic*, if not the unjust rule of a man who himself is tyrannized by his basest desires? Eros is classified by Plato as a demonic force that floats between the human and the divine, helping us to rise or transporting the soul into a life of baseness and suffering in which others suffer with us. The philosopher and the tyrant, the highest and lowest of human types, are linked through some perverse trick of nature by the power of love.

We are no longer accustomed to thinking of eros in this way. Erotic attachment, the life of the mind, the world of politics—for us these are wholly distinct realms operating independently of one another and governed by different laws. We are unprepared, therefore, to understand one of the most extraordinary episodes in the intellectual life of our time, the love and friendship between Martin Heidegger, Hannah Arendt, and Karl Jaspers. These three thinkers first met in the 1920s and were immediately attracted to each other because of a common passion for philosophy. But as they found themselves drawn into the political upheaval that shook Europe, and then the entire world, this passion eventually spilled over into every aspect of their personal lives and political commitments. That in their youth Heidegger and Arendt were briefly carnal lovers turns out to be a detail and not terribly revealing. What is important and deserves serious reflection is how all three came to see the place of passion in the life of the mind and in the allure of modern tyranny.

The affair between Heidegger and Arendt was first reported in Elisabeth Young-Bruehl's absorbing biography, *Hannah Arendt: For Love of the World* (1984), though it received little popular attention at the time, thanks largely to Young-Bruehl's discretion and sense of proportion. A few years ago, however, the affair became the subject of distasteful polemics following the publication of Elżbieta Ettinger's study *Hannah Arendt/Martin Heidegger* (1995). Professor Ettinger hoped to create a scandal with her little book and she succeeded. While working on a biography of Arendt she acquired permission to read the Arendt–Heidegger correspondence, which, under the terms set by the literary executors, few had seen and no one had been allowed to quote from. Having read the letters, Ettinger then rushed an account of the love affair into print, paraphrasing Heidegger's letters at length and quoting directly from Arendt's replies.

Ettinger portrayed the Arendt–Heidegger relationship as a deeply pathological one that stretched from their first encounter in 1924 until Arendt's sudden death in 1975. In this account Heidegger was cast as the ruthless predator who bedded a naive and vulnerable young student, dropped her when it suited his purposes, ignored her plight when she fled Germany in 1933, and then cynically exploited her fame as a Jewish thinker after the war in order to rehabilitate himself and his thought, which had been deeply compromised by his Nazism. As for Arendt, Ettinger saw her as a victim who collaborated in her own humiliation, suffering slights and rejection from Heidegger the man and slaving away to promote Heidegger the thinker, despite his intellectual support of Hitler. Whether Arendt did this out of a deep psychological need for affection from a father figure, out of Jewish self-hatred, or out of a foolish wish to ingratiate herself with a charlatan she mistook for a genius, Ettinger could not decide. So she advanced all three hypotheses, on the basis of her private reading of an incomplete correspondence. From any standpoint, the book was irresponsible.

Still, the scandal was there, and during the months that followed Arendt's critics seized on it as evidence that she was intellectually untrustworthy. Her defenders, who have made her into an object of passionate hagiography in recent years, were not slow to respond but did little to raise the tone. And, most important, few but Professor Ettinger had seen the letters. At this point the executors of the Heidegger and Arendt literary estates stepped in and agreed to publish all the correspondence they possessed in order to put the entire matter before the public. Since Heidegger destroyed all of Arendt's early letters, copies of which she rarely made, this meant that the correspondence would be incomplete and that three quarters of it would come from Heidegger's side. Nonetheless, the decision was made to proceed and we now have the letters in a carefully edited and helpfully annotated German edition.[1] The decision has proved wise, for the published volume does more than set the record straight. It puts the Heidegger–Arendt relationship in a new, and intellectually more significant, setting: the philosophical

---

1. Hannah Arendt and Martin Heidegger, *Briefe 1925 bis 1975 und andere Zeugnisse*, edited by Ursula Ludz (Frankfurt am Main: Klostermann, 1998).

friendship they developed and shared with their mutual friend the existentialist thinker Karl Jaspers.[2]

Martin Heidegger was born in the small town of Messkirch, Baden-Württemberg, in 1889. As a young boy he seemed destined for the priesthood, and in fact at the age of twenty he decided to become a novice in the Society of Jesus. But Heidegger's career as a budding Jesuit lasted only two weeks before he was sent home complaining of chest pains. His interest in religion remained strong, however, and for the next two years he studied at the theological seminary of Freiburg University and contributed occasional articles to somewhat reactionary Catholic periodicals, attacking the cultural decadence of his time. In 1911 he suffered further heart problems and transferred out of the seminary to study mathematics, while devoting himself privately to philosophy.

Heidegger's leave-taking from the intellectual tradition of the Church was extremely drawn out. As late as 1921 he could still write to his student Karl Löwith that he considered himself to be above all "a Christian theologian." Ostensibly, Heidegger was studying with the great phenomenologist Edmund Husserl, who had arrived in Freiburg in 1916 to fulfill his program of

---

2. Over the past fifteen years volumes of both Arendt's and Heidegger's correspondence with Jaspers have been published. The Arendt–Jaspers letters appeared in German in 1985 and were translated as *Hannah Arendt–Karl Jaspers Correspondence, 1926–1969* (Harcourt Brace, 1992). The Heidegger–Jaspers correspondence appeared as *Briefwechsel, 1920–1963* (Frankfurt am Main: Klostermann, 1990) but, inexplicably, has never been translated into English.

scraping the metaphysical barnacles off the philosophical tradition. Husserl, who wished to bring a new rigor to bear on the philosophical examination of consciousness and return it "to the things themselves," was at first reserved toward Heidegger, whom he considered a Catholic thinker. But he began to enjoy his long philosophical conversations with this student, and was disappointed when Heidegger's war service interrupted them. On Heidegger's return, Husserl made him his private assistant, a position he occupied until 1923. In those years the personal relationship between Husserl and Heidegger was a quasi-parental one, as the older scholar groomed his young disciple to replace him.

When Karl Jaspers first met him in 1920, Heidegger was introduced by Mrs. Husserl as her husband's "phenomenological child." It was an encounter fated to transform the lives of both men. Jaspers was six years Heidegger's senior and already a well-known figure in German intellectual life. He had studied law and medicine as a young man and received his *Habilitation* in psychology, which he then taught in Freiburg. His fame rested on a book he published in 1919 called *Psychology of Worldviews*, an idiosyncratic and today virtually unreadable work mired in the technical vocabulary of Max Weber and Wilhelm Dilthey, but which also managed to address existential themes in the manner of Kierkegaard and Nietzsche.

The book eventually earned Jaspers a chair in philosophy, though he, like Heidegger, felt a barely concealed contempt for the university philosophers of his time. The two thinkers soon discovered a common interest in what Jaspers in his book had called "limit situations"—situations in which the cloud of forgetting that normally envelops our *Existenz* evaporates and we are suddenly confronted with the fundamental questions of life and, especially, death. Jaspers described how these situations evoke in us states of anxiety and guilt, yet also open up the possibility of living authentically by confronting them freely and resolutely. Although he was emerging from the very different intellectual traditions of scholasticism and phenomenology, Heidegger was absorbed with these very same issues, which became central themes in his masterwork, *Being and Time* (1927).

Over the next few years the two men developed a deep philosophical friendship, as can been seen in their early exchange of letters. It was cemented in 1922 when Jaspers invited Heidegger to stay with him for a week in Heidelberg (where Jaspers now held his chair). It was an unforgettable experience for both, and thereafter they referred to themselves as a *Kampfgemeinschaft*, comrades in arms. Yet from the start it was also clear that, if the friendship were to survive, it would have to rest on the awkward fact that Heidegger was the superior thinker, and Jaspers, although older and better known than Heidegger, would have to recognize this.

When Heidegger met Jaspers it so happened that he was already drafting a long review of *Psychology of Worldviews*, which he obligingly sent his new friend in 1921. Outwardly, Jaspers was grateful for Heidegger's attention and suggestions, though he professed not to grasp the position from which his friend leveled his criticisms. Inwardly, Jaspers was devastated. For this "review" was nothing less than a manifesto for a new way of thinking for which Jaspers was ill-prepared, and toward which he felt little inclination. After paying his respects to Jaspers's psychological acuity, Heidegger objected in the strongest terms to his "aesthetic" approach to psychological experience, which treated it as an object that could be observed from without, rather than as something we live within. In order to reach what is "primordial" in human existence, Heidegger wrote, philosophy must begin by recognizing that consciousness necessarily exists in time, that it is "historical." Human existence is a certain kind of "being," different from the "being" of mere objects, Heidegger claimed: to say "I am" is to assert something altogether different from asserting "it is." That is because I "am" through a process of historical self-enactment in which I experience "anxious care" about my existence, which I must take over and possess for myself if I am to live authentically. All these concepts first articulated in the review of Jaspers—"primordiality," "being," "historicity," "anxiety," and "care"—soon found their way into *Being and Time*.

The friendship survived Heidegger's crushing review and even deepened over the next few years, despite a few rocky patches. Yet Jaspers was haunted by the sense that Heidegger, and only Heidegger, had seen through him and understood "what I failed to achieve," as he once wrote in a private notebook. From that point on Heidegger served as the standard by which Jaspers judged his own philosophical seriousness, and the stimulus for moody reflections about the advantages and disadvantages of philosophy for life. That we know because we have this notebook, an extraordinary three-hundred-page manuscript of assembled reflections on Heidegger which Jaspers collected from 1928 until at least 1964, and which was found on his desk after his death.[3] These notes oscillate between expressions of wonder ("he seems to notice what no one else saw"), frustration ("communicationless, worldless, godless"), and loyalty ("none of the other living philosophers can interest me"). Jaspers even records a dream in which, during a tense conversation with some of Heidegger's critics, his friend suddenly approached and addressed him for the first time with the familiar *du*. The two then set off together, alone.

In 1923 Heidegger moved to Marburg to take up his first independent academic position, and there drew a following of students who traveled from the four corners of Europe to study with him. One of those was Hannah Arendt, who years later in her commemorative essay "Martin Heidegger at Eighty" (1969) described in The New York Review of Books the excitement her entire generation felt about him, in sentences that have now become famous:

> There was hardly more than a name, but the name traveled all over Germany like the rumor of the hidden king.... The rumor about Heidegger

---

3. This manuscript has appeared in a German volume edited by Hans Saner, titled *Notizen zu Martin Heidegger* (Munich: Piper, second edition, 1989).

put it quite simply: Thinking has come to life again; the cultural treasures of the past, believed to be dead, are being made to speak, in the course of which it turns out that they propose things altogether different from the familiar, worn-out trivialities they had been presumed to say. There exists a teacher; one can perhaps learn to think.[4]

Hannah Arendt was born in Königsberg, East Prussia, in 1906 and was only eighteen years old when she arrived in Marburg. As a young woman she had read some Kant but much more Kierkegaard, who was the thinker young Germans turned to after the disaster of World War I. What made Kierkegaard so attractive was his passion, which stood in such stark contrast to the bourgeois self-satisfaction of the Wilhelmine era and the arid speculations of the philosophical schools then dominant in Germany. It was this passion that Arendt, like Jaspers, immediately remarked in Heidegger, and which she could still recall in 1969:

What was experienced was that thinking as pure activity—and this means impelled neither by the thirst for knowledge nor by the drive for cognition—can become a passion which not so much rules and oppresses all other capacities and gifts, as it orders them and prevails through them. We are so accustomed to the old opposition of reason

---

4. "Martin Heidegger at Eighty," *The New York Review of Books*, October 21, 1971.

versus passion, spirit versus life, that the idea of a passionate thinking, in which thinking and aliveness become one, takes us somewhat aback.

She then added, in a very Platonic turn of phrase:

> Also, the passion of thinking, like the other passions, seizes the person—seizes those qualities of the individual of which the sum, when ordered by the will, amounts to what we commonly call "character"—takes possession of him and, as it were, annihilates his "character" which cannot hold its own against this onslaught.

We get a sense of the intellectual passion Heidegger generated by reading the lectures he gave when Arendt first arrived in Marburg.[5] The ostensible aim of the lecture course was to develop a commentary on Plato's dialogue concerning philosophy and pseudophilosophy, the *Sophist*. In Heidegger's hands, however, the craft of commentary became a means of recovering what he took to be the dialogue's deepest problems and confronting them directly. In the *Sophist*, Heidegger saw two overriding issues. The first was ontological: the problem of Being—a term sometimes capitalized in English to indicate that Heidegger does not mean the

---

5. The lectures from the 1924–1925 winter semester were published in German in 1992 and have recently appeared in English as *Plato's Sophist*, translated by Richard Rojcewicz and André Schuwer (Indiana University Press, 1997).

fact that there are particular entities or beings, but rather what might be called their "beingness," or Being. "Why is there beingness/Being rather than nothingness?" is a question the *Sophist* makes us ask. The second problem in the dialogue was the correct definition of truth, which Heidegger interpreted to be a process of "disclosure" or "uncovering" of what entities are rather than a correspondence between concept and object, as philosophers from Plato onward held. His commentary on the dialogue then turns into a masterful explication of these problems and how a new approach, deriving from phenomenology, might reveal novel answers to them. It was this audacity that made Plato and Aristotle seem suddenly alive and vital to Arendt and her classmates—and, more subtly, also made Heidegger appear as their only legitimate heir.

Heidegger's and Arendt's passion for each other bloomed sometime during the course of this semester, and by the time their published correspondence begins in February 1925 it was clear that some sort of step had been taken:

10.II.25

Dear Miss Arendt,

I must return to you tonight and speak to your heart.

Everything should be simple, clear, and pure between us. Only then will we be worthy of an encounter. That you were my student and I your teacher only provided the occasion for what happened between us.

I will never be able to possess you, but from now on you will belong to my life, which shall increase through you....

The path your young life will take is hidden. We will submit to it. And my faithfulness should only help you be true to yourself....

The gift of our friendship becomes a duty, through which we will grow. A duty that permits me to ask forgiveness for having forgotten myself for a moment during our walk.

Still, I must thank you and, in a kiss on your pure forehead, take the integrity of your essence into my work.

      Be happy, good one!

      Your

        M. H.

Within the month another threshold had been passed:

                        27.II.25

Dear Hannah,

The demonic has seized me. The still, prayer-like folding of your loving hands and your gleaming forehead guarded it through womanly transfiguration.

The like has never happened to me before.

In the rainstorm on the way home you were even more beautiful and great. And I would have liked to walk with you for nights on end.

As a symbol of my thanks, take this little book. It will also serve as a symbol of this semester.

Please, Hannah, give me just a few words. I can't just let you leave like that.

You must be in a rush before your trip, but just a few words, not "beautifully" written.

Just as you write. Only that you have written them.

Your

M.

The correspondence continues in this vein for many passion-filled months. Heidegger's letters to Arendt are filled with romantic commonplaces—fields of flowers, ruined towers, professions of guilt and self-renunciation —mixed with philosophical ruminations and sensible professional advice. Although we have none of her earliest letters, we have a copy of a short, and very melancholy, autobiographical text called "Shadows," which she sent to him that April. It describes a young woman who had already suffered through many unsatisfactory moods in her short life, passing from the conviction that *Sehnsucht*—yearning—could be an end in itself to a growing anxiety about the meaning of life. Now she had finally arrived at the stage where she could offer "unbending devotion" to one person alone—a bittersweet devotion, however, fully aware that "all things come to an end." Heidegger responded to this cri de cœur like the mature lover he was, assuring Arendt that "from now on you live wrapped up in my work," and reminding her that "there are only 'shadows' where there is sun."

Was Heidegger the predator and Arendt the victim in this romance, as Professor Ettinger would have us believe? Was this high-minded philosophical cooing merely a cover for sexual domination? On the contrary, the mature reader of these letters will be struck by the touching authenticity they express, in what was, after all, a rather conventional drama heading for its predictable end. The married older professor and his younger student write to each other about the nature of love and about what she should study. They exchange poems and pictures, listen to music when they are alone, and even decide to read *The Magic Mountain* together, speculating about the doomed love of Madame Chauchat and Hans Castorp. Heidegger also writes touchingly of his love of nature and how it merges with his love for Arendt:

> Todtnauberg, 21.III.25
>
> Dear Hannah,
>
> It is a marvelous winter up here, so I've had some wonderful, refreshing trips....
>
> I often hope that you are doing as well as I am here. The solitude of the mountains, the quiet life of the mountain people, the elemental nearness of sun, storm, and heavens, the simplicity of an abandoned trail on a wide and deeply snow-covered slope—all this keeps the soul far, far removed from all unfocused and moody existence....
>
> When the storm is howling outside the cabin, then I remember "our storm," or I take a quiet walk along the Lahn River, or I dream about a young girl in a raincoat, her hat pulled down

over her large, quiet eyes, who entered my office
for the first time, shy and reserved, giving every
question a short reply—and then I transpose the
picture to the last day of the semester—and then
I know for sure, that life is history.

> I hold you dear,
> Your
> Martin

Inevitably, Arendt rebels against the constraints of
their forbidden love and complains that she is being
ignored; Heidegger pleads guilty but tries to make her
understand his need for isolation to work on the project that eventually became *Being and Time*. Then, in a
coup de force, Arendt announces in early 1926 her decision to leave Marburg for Heidelberg, where she will
finish her studies with none other than Karl Jaspers, a
decision Heidegger approves of. Yet six months later
Arendt's will breaks and she writes to him again, and
he responds by suggesting another meeting. For the
next two years they stage rendezvous in hotels or small
towns whenever he is traveling, thereby avoiding detec-
tion. More letters, pictures, and poems pass between
them, along with suggestions from Heidegger for further reading (especially Knut Hamsun).

In 1927 Heidegger published *Being and Time* to
great acclaim and the following year received the call to
Husserl's chair in philosophy in Freiburg. At this point
Arendt decided to make what turned out to be the final
break, which she announces in the first letter we have
in her hand. "I love you as on the first day—that you

know," she writes, and she assures him that her decision has only been made to protect that love from the reality of the situation. Within a year she would enter into an ill-advised marriage to Günther Stern, a former Husserl student, and move with him to Frankfurt. How Heidegger reacted to this news we do not know. What we do know, from a letter Arendt sent him in 1930, is that she and Stern eventually visited Heidegger together and that this encounter brought back a flood of painful emotions. "The sight of you aroused my knowledge of the clearest and most important continuity of my life, and—let me please say it—of the continuity of our love." Yet when, for some reason, Heidegger departs with Stern by train, and fails to recognize Arendt standing on the platform, she is left heartbroken and alone. "As always," she writes, "there is nothing for me but resignation, and waiting, waiting, waiting." She would wait another two decades before seeing Heidegger again.

Over the next few years the lives of the three friends and lovers advanced independently without major incident. In 1929 Hannah Arendt published a doctoral thesis under Jaspers, *Love and Saint Augustine*, a work inspired in more than one sense by her encounter with Heidegger. She then set to work on a biography of Rahel Varnhagen, a book that would not see the light of day until the 1950s.[6] Karl Jaspers wrote and published prolifically on everything from psychology to

---

6. *Love and Saint Augustine* (University of Chicago Press, 1996); *Rahel Varnhagen: The Life of a Jewess* (Johns Hopkins University Press, 1997).

religion to Nietzsche, though with decreasing philosophical ambition since receiving Heidegger's review.
As for Heidegger himself, the late Weimar years saw
him at the peak of his intellectual power and influence.
In 1929 he was invited to Davos, Switzerland, to
debate the respected neo-Kantian philosopher Ernst
Cassirer, and so successfully trounced him in the eyes of
young people in the audience that the mantle of leading
German philosopher was unofficially bestowed upon
him there. He received it officially shortly thereafter in
1930 when the German government made him the first
of two offers of the philosophy chair at Berlin, the most
prestigious in the country, which he turned down.
Although Heidegger had given up his plan to write a
second volume of *Being and Time*, he did publish fragments from it, beginning with a substantial and still
essential work, *Kant and the Problem of Metaphysics*,
that had already appeared in 1929. And in his lectures
he continued to go ever deeper into "the question of
Being."

The letters Jaspers and Heidegger exchanged during these years reflect a genuine friendship, if a less
intense one now that both were busy, established professors. In his short *Philosophical Autobiography*
Jaspers described his feelings as a mix of wonder and
nagging concern:

> Through Heidegger I saw in a contemporary that
> "something" that normally can be found only in
> the past, and that is essential to philosophiz-
> ing. . . . I saw his depth, yet also found something

else that I couldn't quite put my finger on, something difficult to take.... It could sometimes seem
that a demon had crept into him.... Over the
decades there grew up a tension between affection
and alienation, wonder at his abilities and rejection of his incomprehensible foolishness, a feeling
of sharing a foundation of philosophizing and a
trace of a completely different attitude toward me.[7]

Whatever his doubts, Jaspers still had confidence in
Heidegger's character and in the promise of his philosophical work, at least enough to have encouraged Heidegger to seize the moment of his fame and to play a
more active part in reforming the university. In 1931 he
wrote to Heidegger that "it appears that, in the long run,
the philosophy of the German universities is in your
hands," an assessment Heidegger obviously shared.

As is now well known, in April 1933 Martin Heidegger left his Black Forest cabin to become rector of
Freiburg University, joining the Nazi Party in May, and
held the position until the following April. For many
years Heidegger's air-brushed account of this period
was widely accepted; many were convinced that he
had accepted the post unwillingly, had tried to limit
the damage done to scholarship, protected Jews, was
relieved to give up the office—and, most important,

---

7. *Philosophische Autobiographie* (Munich: Piper, second edition, 1984),
pp. 95, 97–98. Jaspers wrote this short volume in 1953 but deleted the chapter on Heidegger, from which these citations are taken, just before it was published. The chapter has been inserted into the second edition.

quickly lost his illusion of national renewal through Nazism. But during the past two decades enough has been uncovered to establish a well-documented and generally accepted account of what really happened.[8] It is now clear that Heidegger had voiced support for the Nazis at least since the end of 1931; that he campaigned actively for the rectorship; that, once appointed, he threw all his energies into "revolutionizing" the university and gave propaganda lectures across Germany, ending them with the standard "Heil Hitler!"

His personal behavior was no less despicable. He cut off relations with all his Jewish colleagues, including his mentor Edmund Husserl. (In the early Forties he even removed the dedication to Husserl in *Being and Time* and later just as silently restored it.) Heidegger also used his considerable powers to denounce on political grounds, in secret letters to Nazi officials, a colleague, the future Nobel chemist Hermann Staudinger, and a former student, Eduard Baumgarten. And even after resigning his post, Heidegger signed petitions in support of Hitler and lobbied the regime to allow him to establish a philosophical academy in Berlin. In 1936, two years after his resignation, Karl Löwith saw him in

---

8. Among the many useful works on this subject are Victor Farías, *Heidegger and Nazism* (Temple University Press, 1989); Hugo Ott, *Martin Heidegger: A Political Life* (Basic Books, 1993); Günther Neske and Emil Kettering, editors, *Martin Heidegger and National Socialism* (Paragon House, 1990); Richard Wolin, editor, *The Heidegger Controversy: A Critical Reader* (MIT Press, 1993). See also Thomas Sheehan, "Heidegger and the Nazis," *The New York Review of Books*, June 16, 1988, and "A Normal Nazi," *The New York Review of Books*, January 14, 1993.

Rome, where he wore a Nazi lapel pin and explained to his former student how concepts in *Being and Time* had inspired his political engagement.

To his later chagrin, Jaspers reacted lethargically to Heidegger's political turn, even though Hannah Arendt had warned him of its significance. In 1933 she fled to Paris with her husband and began working for various Jewish relief agencies. Just before leaving she evidently sent Heidegger a scathing letter confronting him with rumors that he was in the grip of a "raging anti-Semitism" and was excluding Jewish students from his seminars—charges that were inexact but prophetic.[9] He testily denied all these charges, yet within months he was in the rector's chair.

Arendt spent the next seven years living hand-to-mouth in France before being forced to flee yet again, this time to the United States. She arrived in New York City in 1941 as the war spread across Europe and then she lost touch completely with both Heidegger and Jaspers. Jaspers, however, stayed in contact with Heidegger for a while. In March 1933, shortly after the Nazis took power, Heidegger visited Jaspers in Heidelberg and they spent the visit amiably enough, listening to recordings of Gregorian chant and discussing philosophy. When the conversation turned, inevitably, to politics, Heidegger would only say, "One must get involved."

---

9. While Heidegger did not explicitly exclude Jewish students, beginning in 1934 he declined to direct their theses and sent them to a Catholic colleague instead.

In May he was back in Heidelberg, now as the Freiburg rector, delivering a harangue to students about the Nazis' plans for the university. Jaspers sat in the front row scowling, his hands in his pockets. After they returned to Jaspers's house Jaspers tried to draw Heidegger out, remarking that surely his friend could not agree with the Nazis on the Jewish question. Heidegger: "But there is a dangerous international network of Jews." Jaspers: "How can such an un-cultivated man like Adolf Hitler govern Germany?" Heidegger: "Culture doesn't matter. Just look at his marvelous hands." Heidegger left early and never saw his old friend again.

Jaspers was stunned. Nothing Heidegger ever said to him before had prepared him for this rapid political engagement with Nazism, and in his *Philosophical Autobiography* Jaspers blames himself for failing to keep his friend from "sliding off the rails." For the next three years he continued to write occasionally to Heidegger, both during and after the rectorship. Shortly before his last visit to Jaspers, Heidegger had delivered his infamous *Rektoratsrede* (Rectoral Address), in which he explicitly placed his technical philosophical vocabulary in the service of the Nazi takeover of the university. The published address was enormously popular, despite its obscurity. (On receiv-ing a copy, Karl Löwith later reported, he wondered whether it meant he was supposed to study the pre-Socratics or march with the storm troopers.) But Jaspers tried to find good things to say about it, writing that "my trust in your philosophy, which I have more strongly since our conversations earlier this year, is not destroyed through qualities of this address that only reflect the times." The two estranged friends continued to exchange books and notes until 1937, when Jaspers was removed from his post and forced into the terrifying position of surviving until the war's end as an anti-Nazi married to a Jewish woman and barred from leaving the country. He and his wife carried poison capsules with them at all times, just in case.

Heidegger's service as Freiburg's rector lasted barely a year. But his fateful decision in favor of Nazism posed profound problems that would absorb Jaspers and Arendt for the rest of their lives. Jaspers was a friend, Arendt had been a lover, and both admired Heidegger as the thinker who had, so they believed, single-handedly revived genuine philosophizing. Now they had to ask themselves whether his political decision reflected only a weakness of character, or whether it had been prepared for by what Arendt would later call his "passionate thinking." If the latter, did that mean that their own intellectual/erotic attachment to him as a thinker was tainted? Had they been mistaken only about Heidegger or also about philosophy itself and its relation to political reality?

Whether Heidegger posed these sorts of questions to himself is difficult to know. Apart from his experience as rector, he was not in the habit of taking public positions, and his published writings, including his 1927 masterwork *Being and Time*, were not transparently political. However, after the war, many of his readers—among them Jaspers and Arendt—began to see that

Heidegger's treatment of fundamental existential themes in *Being and Time* did point to a way of understanding political matters, and even acting upon them, from a new, suprapolitical perspective. And it was from this perspective that Heidegger had seen in Nazism the birth of a new, and better, world.

The term "world" is a central one in the philosophical vocabulary Heidegger began developing in *Being and Time*. There he portrayed human beings as thrown by historical destiny into a coherent realm of activity, language, and thought he called a "world." This world is the product of fate, not of nature; it arises out of what Heidegger would later call a mysterious "event" in which Being (*Sein*) finds a place (a "there," *da*) in which to unveil itself, a place inhabited by human beings (*Dasein*). Being is not a transcendent realm that can be reached only (if at all) by rising above human experience; for Heidegger, whatever Being is, it only comes to light in relation to human "worlds." Each civilization or culture is a "world" for Heidegger. Thus there is the Western "world," but also the "world" of the carpenter, or the peasant.

Human beings, however, inhabit their worlds within the horizon of time: they inherit traditions from the past, project themselves into the future, and die. Heidegger's reasoning is that if Being only reveals itself in human worlds, and those are shaped by temporality, then Being must be dependent on time, too. And that would mean that Being has no other meaning than temporality: the unfolding of things in time.

Heidegger arrives at this conclusion in *Being and*

Time by means of a subtle and quite powerful analysis of the temporal human condition and how man tries to flee it. In Heidegger's view, man has a tendency to lose himself in his world and "forget" his mortality, and by extension that of his world. He falls in with the crowd (the "they"), engages in idle chatter, lets himself be absorbed by average everydayness—all in order to avoid the fundamental question of his existence and its responsibility. We are inauthentic creatures: "Everyone is other, and no one is himself." Authenticity is not easy to recover, however. It requires a new "orientation," Heidegger claims, a confrontation with our finitude, an "authentic being-toward-death." It would mean heeding the call of conscience, exhibiting "care" toward the manifestation of Being. And, above all, it would demand a new "resoluteness," which signifies "letting oneself be summoned out of one's lostness in the 'they.'"

Heidegger's rhetoric of authenticity and resoluteness has been interpreted in various ways. The canonical interpretation has it that *Being and Time* is primarily a work of ontology, an inquiry into the nature of existence, and beyond that just a summons to become what we are: to assume without self-deceit the full responsibility of being finite human creatures. Others have seen in this work a profound hostility to the modern world and a yearning for a new historical epoch to be brought about through human resolve, the creation of a more authentic "world" attentive to the call of Being. And if, as Heidegger sometimes implies, "worlds" are cultural or even national wholes, that would make *Being and*

Time a program for national regeneration—which is precisely what Heidegger would see in National Socialism a few years after this work was published.

There are notorious problems with both these interpretations, and they are compounded by a shift in Heidegger's thinking and rhetoric that began in the Thirties and continued in his postwar writings. Beginning in this period Heidegger moved from a phenomenological analysis of the link between *Sein* and *Dasein*, undertaken from the standpoint of human existence, to a new analysis of it that he claimed took the standpoint of Being itself—whatever that meant. He also began writing, in a self-fashioned mythopoetic language inspired by Hölderlin, about Being as a divinity revealing itself to man. Whether this shift represented a change of Heidegger's mind or simply a second, complementary part of a lifelong task (as he insisted) is a serious question. And it obscures further what, if any, political teaching Heidegger was trying to deliver through his philosophy, and how he eventually came to view his own resolute leap into contemporary history.

Having made this shift, the later Heidegger speaks less about resoluteness and authenticity, more about learning to "let Being be" and adopting an attitude of *Gelassenheit*, Meister Eckhart's term for serene renunciation. As time went on he presented himself not as a proponent of existential decision and self-assertion, but on the contrary as the most profound critic of the Western "nihilism" that had come to sanction such willfulness and had produced fascism, communism,

modern democracy, and technology, all of which Heidegger considered nihilistic.

Still, even his *Gelassenheit* had a passionate, urgent
quality to it. Heidegger never ceased to describe modern man as living on a precipice, poised to fall into
either complete oblivion of Being or a new "world"
where the meaning of Being would again be uncovered;
he must move or he will be moved by a historical force
stronger than himself. In his manuscripts of the
Thirties, which are slowly appearing in his collected
works in German, there is much made of "the preparation of the appearance of the last god." In some of
them we do indeed find contemptuous remarks about
the Nazis' blind self-assertion and their feeble attempts
to construct a "folk philosophy"—though Heidegger
seems intent on going the Nazis one better. It is not
just any people that founds a philosophy, he writes at
one point, but rather "the philosophy of a people is one
that makes the people into a people of a philosophy."
Was his own philosophy aimed at doing just that?

In reading the later Heidegger one cannot escape the
impression that, despite his experience, he was never
able to confront the issue of philosophy's relation to
politics, of philosophical passion to political passion.
For him, this was not the issue; he simply had been
fooled into thinking that the Nazis' resolve to found a
new nation was compatible with his private and loftier
resolution to refound the entire tradition of Western
thought, and thereby Western existence. Heidegger
considered himself a victim of Nazism—hence his
astonishing remark to Ernst Jünger that he would only

apologize for his Nazi past if Hitler could be brought back to apologize to him.

Heidegger finally decided that the Nazis themselves had destroyed the "inner truth and greatness" of National Socialism, and that by not following Heidegger's path they had kept the Germans from their rendezvous with destiny. Now all was lost; Being had withdrawn and was nowhere to be found. All that remained was the spreading spiritual desert of modern technology and modern politics. In such circumstances the genuine thinker could only flee to his study, get his thinking straight, and wait in serene expectation for a new, messianic epoch of Being. In the famous phrase he uttered during his interview with *Der Spiegel* in the Sixties, "Only a god can save us now."

Heidegger emerged from the war a broken man and even spent time in a sanatorium to recover his forces. When the French occupied Freiburg in 1945 they threatened to take his library and called him before a denazification commission, which eventually decided to ban him from teaching and even, temporarily, withdrew his pension. In a vain effort to save himself Heidegger proposed that the commission seek a deposition from his friend Karl Jaspers, who, he hoped, would still vouch for him.

Jaspers, it turned out, had spent much of the war brooding about the Heidegger case and was now prepared to offer a sober and morally astute judgment on it. In his friend's defense he claimed that, as far as he knew, Heidegger was never an anti-Semite in the Twenties, and that his behavior thereafter was inconsistent in this respect. (We now know this to be incorrect.[10]) Jaspers also tried to explain that Heidegger's intellectualized Nazism had little to do with the real thing; he was an unpolitical man, Jaspers wrote, more like a child who got his finger stuck in the wheel of history. Yet although Heidegger was "perhaps unique among contemporary German philosophers" in his seriousness, and therefore should be allowed to write and publish, teaching was another matter. "Heidegger's manner of thinking," Jaspers concluded, "which to me seems in its essence unfree, dictatorial, and incapable of communication, would today be in its pedagogical effects disastrous," especially since "his manner of speaking and his actions have a certain affinity with National Socialist characteristics." The commission followed Jaspers's advice and imposed a teaching ban that lasted until 1950.

This did not mean that Jaspers was prepared to wash his hands of his friend. On the contrary, he also expressed to the commission his hope that Heidegger would experience an "authentic rebirth" in the future. At the time Jaspers was convinced that Heidegger's failings were essentially those of a weak *Luftmensch*, not of his philosophy, and that if he could be made to understand his responsibilities, Heidegger the philosopher

---

10. Ten years ago a recommendation letter from 1929 surfaced, in which Heidegger stated that Germany needed more scholars rooted in its "soil" and complained of the "Judaization" of intellectual life. This letter was in support of the unfortunate Eduard Baumgarten, whom Heidegger would later turn against. See Ulrich Sieg, "Die Verjudung des deutschen Geistes," *Die Zeit*, December 22, 1989, p. 50.

might be saved. This Christian redemption motif also appears in Jaspers's letters to Arendt, in which he muses on the fact that Heidegger "has knowledge of something that hardly anyone notices these days," yet his "impure soul" needed to undergo a complete revolution. Arendt was more than a little skeptical about conversion myths but did agree that Heidegger "lives in depths and with a passion one does not easily forget."

In his *Philosophical Autobiography* and *Notes on Martin Heidegger* Jaspers speaks of his personal sense of culpability for having failed to warn his friend about the mistake he was making in 1933. After the war, Jaspers hoped to effect a genuine, yet morally defensible, rapprochement that would salvage whatever of philosophical value remained in his friend. But how? The occasion finally presented itself in 1948 when Jaspers moved to Basel, Switzerland, where he was to spend the remainder of his life. He wrote a letter to Heidegger in March of that year but could not bring himself to send it, then wrote another the following February. "I have long waited to write to you," he begins, "and today, on a Sunday morning, I finally feel the impulse." Jaspers is brutally direct, confessing that the moment he learned of Heidegger's secret denunciation of his own student Eduard Baumgarten was "one of the most decisive experiences of my life." He also reports on his 1945 letter to the denazification commission, making no excuses for what it contained.

None of what has passed can be forgotten, he writes, yet he still wonders if some sort of philosophical and even personal relationship might be possible, since "whatever is philosophy must be bound together in origin and aim." He concludes, "I greet you out of a distant past, over an abyss of time, holding fast to something that once was and cannot be nothing." Heidegger responded to this expression of philosophical comradeship with gratitude, and for the next year a flurry of letters passed between them, as did copies of writings that, by that point, reflected utterly different approaches to thinking.

The whole subject of Nazism was avoided until Heidegger finally addressed it himself in March 1950 and tried to explain why he stopped seeing the Jaspers family after 1933. I was not silent because your wife is Jewish, he declares, "but simply because I was ashamed." Jaspers was touched by this expression of shame, which he took as a promising sign of repentance, telling him that in those dark years Heidegger was a child incapable of understanding what he was doing. The matter might have rested there, had Heidegger not chosen to respond with shameless self-justifications and irresponsible political speculations. He seizes on the image of himself as an innocent child and admits that when the Jews and leftists were threatened in the Thirties they were more clearsighted than he had been. But now it is Germany's turn to suffer, Heidegger complains, and no one but he seems to care. It is surrounded by enemies on every side and Stalin is on the march, though "people" choose not to notice. Modern man puts his faith in the political realm, which is dead and now occupied by technological and economic calculation. All we can hope, Heidegger concludes, is that a hidden "advent" will burst forth out of the Germans' new homelessness (*Heimatslosigkeit*).

34

Jaspers waited two years to respond to this bizarre diatribe, which finally drove him to the conclusion that Heidegger was irredeemable—as a man and as a thinker. Heidegger was no longer for him the model of what a philosopher could be, but rather a demonic antiphilosopher consumed by dangerous fantasies. And so he lashed out with passion at the man he once loved:

> A philosophy that speculates and speaks in sentences like those in your letter, that evokes the vision of something monstrous, isn't it in fact another preparation of the victory of totalitarianism, in that it separates itself from reality? Just as the philosophy circulating before 1933 helped prepare the acceptance of Hitler? Is something similar going on here? . . .
>
> Can the political, which you consider played out, ever disappear? Hasn't it only changed its forms and means? And mustn't one actually recognize them?

He then turned to Heidegger's hope for an "advent":

> My horror grew when I read that. As far as I can see that is utter dreaming, like so much dreaming that—always at the "right" historical moment— has fooled us over the last fifty years. Do you really intend to step out as a prophet revealing

the supernatural from hidden sources, as a
philosopher seduced away from reality?

Heidegger never responded to a single one of these
questions. Occasional notes bearing birthday greetings
would pass between them for another decade, but the
friendship was over.

As Heidegger's friendship with Jaspers dissolved, a
new one began to develop with Hannah Arendt, much
to Jaspers's surprise. In 1946 Arendt published an article titled "What Is Existential Philosophy?" in *Partisan
Review*, and there she pronounced Heidegger's philosophy to be an unintelligible form of "superstition." As
for his Nazism, she refused to attribute it to a mere lack
of character, preferring instead to blame his incorrigi-
ble romanticism, "a spiritual playfulness that stems in
part from delusions of grandeur and in part from
despair." When told by Jaspers that Heidegger as rector had not banned his teacher Husserl from the university, as Arendt had reported, she still maintained
(again mistakenly) that Heidegger had signed an official circular to that effect. And since "this signature
almost killed [Husserl], I cannot but regard Heidegger
as a potential murderer."[11] For her, it seemed, Heidegger was a closed book.

Yet just before her monumental *Origins of Totalitarianism* appeared in 1951, Arendt made an extended

---

11. As it happened, Heidegger's predecessor signed the decree, which was
subsequently rescinded by the government during Heidegger's tenure. See
Ott, *Martin Heidegger: A Political Life*, pp. 176–177.

trip to Europe, including Germany, on a mission for the Jewish Cultural Reconstruction agency. During these many months she visited her beloved teacher Karl Jaspers, whom she had not seen in seventeen years. There in Basel he showed her his correspondence with Heidegger, and she finally confessed her youthful affair with him. Jaspers responded to this news with a droll, "Ach, but that is very interesting," much to Arendt's relief. Then it became possible for the two of them to discuss the man they once loved, each in his own way.

As chance would have it, Arendt's mission took her to Freiburg in February 1950. She arrived at her hotel, unpacked her suitcase—and promptly sent a note to Heidegger's house announcing her arrival. Heidegger, stunned, wrote an immediate reply inviting her to visit, then set out on foot to deliver it himself. On arriving at the hotel and discovering that Arendt was in, he asked to be announced. This was her reaction, recorded in a letter she sent him two days later:

> This evening and morning are the confirmation of an entire life. . . . When the waiter announced your name . . . it was as if suddenly time stood still. . . . The force of my impulse, after [Hugo] Friedrich gave me your address, mercifully saved me from committing the only truly unforgivable disloyalty and mishandling of my life. . . . Had I done so, it would only have been out of pride, that is, out of a pure, plain, crazy stupidity. Not for any reason.

How could their first meeting in seventeen years be the confirmation of a life? What kind of life? Elżbieta Ettinger would have us believe that Arendt was bewitched by the man who once deflowered her and felt confirmed merely in her youthful romantic attachment. But to her second husband, Heinrich Blücher, Arendt wrote that "we really spoke to one another, it seemed to me, for the first time in our lives"—confirming the existence of a deeper bond in thought and conversation.

The first meetings were by no means easy, not least because of Heidegger's wife, Elfride, who by then was au courant and bore Arendt an understandably intense grudge. But soon letters, gifts, and poems began to crisscross the Atlantic as the former lovers tried to establish a friendship on a new basis, and in the presence of an unwilling and suspicious third party. Over the next year Heidegger became uncharacteristically prolix, sending Arendt seventeen letters and thirty-two poems, with titles such as "You," "The Woman from Afar," "Death," "November 1924" (the date of their first meeting), and "Twenty-five Years" (the period since). He also freely expressed the apocalyptic views about the postwar world that led to the break with Jaspers. He claimed to have discovered the source of the German catastrophe by the mid-Thirties, and to have incorporated his findings into his work— on Heraclitus and Parmenides. Now he expected a civil war to bring Germany and Europe to an end. "The world is becoming bleaker," he wrote in 1952, "...and the essence of history ever more mysterious.... Only resignation remains. Still, despite growing external threats in everything, I see the arrival of new—or, better yet—old 'secrets.' "

Since we do not have Arendt's letters to Heidegger from the Fifties we do not know how she responded to this torrent. She seems to have complained to Jaspers that she found it difficult to be entirely open in her letters to Heidegger and that no general understanding of the essential matter—the Nazi period— would be possible. Jaspers agreed, explaining that Heidegger "really doesn't know and is hardly in a position to find out what devil drove him to do what he did." Heidegger clearly hoped Arendt would effect a reunion between him and Jaspers—"you are the real 'and' between Jaspers and Heidegger"—but that proved impossible. (Indeed, Arendt wrote to her husband that in 1956 Jaspers had delivered an "ultimatum" demanding that she break off contact with Heidegger, but she refused.)

As the Fifties progressed Heidegger's philosophical reputation began to rise again, especially as new works reflecting his philosophical shift began to emerge. Until the mid-Fifties Arendt continued to visit the Heideggers whenever she was in Europe, sent them gifts, and even began arranging for the English translation of *Being and Time*. But the intensity of their reunion began to diminish, whether because Heidegger no longer needed her, or because she felt too inhibited by what remained unspoken. Yet she never lost sight of her intellectual debt to Heidegger, which became increasingly evident in her mature works. When her most philosophically ambitious book, *The Human*

Condition, appeared in German as *Vita Activa* in 1960, she had it sent to Heidegger with the following note:

> You will see that this book bears no dedication. Had things between us turned out right—I mean between us, not with me or you—I would have asked if I might dedicate it to you. It grew directly out of the first Freiburg [*sic*] days and, in that respect, owes everything to you. The way things stand, this seems to me impossible; yet in some way I wanted to tell you at least how things really stand.

She then drafted the following dedication on a separate page and placed it in her files:

> *Re Vita Activa*
> *This book's dedication has been left out.*
> *How should I dedicate it to you,*
> *To the most trusted one,*
> *To whom I remained true*
> *And untrue*
> *And both in love.*

Heidegger never responded to *The Human Condition*, and this wounded Arendt deeply. As she later wrote to Jaspers, it was as if he were punishing her for having asserted herself as a thinker, and she was probably right about this. But his silence is more comprehensible if we take into account what she was trying to achieve in that work. It was, in ways he must have understood, a declaration of independence from central aspects of his philosophy, especially his silence about the relation between politics and philosophy. By defending the dignity of the public *vita activa* against the overweening claims of the private *vita contemplativa*, Arendt was trying to plant a hedge between pure philosophy and thinking about politics, which demanded its own vocabulary and obeyed its own rules.

When Arendt was introduced as a "philosopher" in a 1964 interview for German television she interrupted the interviewer to say, "I'm afraid I have to protest. I do not belong to the circle of philosophers. My profession, if one can speak of it at all, is political theory. I neither feel like a philosopher, nor do I believe that I have been accepted into the circle of philosophers." This was not false modesty on her part; she had come to the conclusion that there is an inescapable tension between the lives of philosophy and politics, and she wished to examine the latter, as she put it, "with eyes unclouded by philosophy."

When pressed on this point she explained that intellectuals generally have trouble thinking clearly about politics, in large part because they see ideas at work in everything. German intellectuals in the Thirties, she told the interviewer, "made up ideas about Hitler, in part terrifically interesting things! Completely interesting and fascinating things! Things far above the ordinary level! I find that grotesque." And when she added that such thinkers inevitably become "trapped in their own ideas," she was obviously thinking about Heidegger. In fact, in her private notebooks she once wrote a

short fable, called "Heidegger the Fox," in which she
described him as a pitiful creature trapped in the lair of
his ideas, convinced it was the entire world:

> Once upon a time there was a fox who was so
> lacking in slyness that he not only kept getting
> caught in traps but couldn't even tell the differ-
> ence between a trap and a non-trap.... He built a
> trap as his burrow.... "So many are visiting me in
> my trap that I have become the best of all foxes."
> And there is some truth in that, too: nobody
> knows the nature of traps better than one who
> sits in a trap his whole life long.

Heidegger remained in his lair another five years
before deigning to communicate with Arendt, sending
her a short note of thanks for her greetings on his
seventy-fifth birthday. In it he paid her a backhanded
compliment, declaring that "despite all her recent pub-
lications" he still considered her to be true to philosophy's calling. But the ice was definitively broken in
1967, when she went to Freiburg to deliver a lecture
and discovered, to her surprise, that Heidegger was
standing in the back of the room. She then began her
remarks by welcoming him before the large (and presumably hostile) audience, and he was touched. From
that moment until Arendt's sudden death in 1975 they
remained close. She once again made annual pilgrim-
ages to Freiburg, took long walks with her former
teacher and discussed the nature of language with him,
and worked intensively on the English translation of

his writings. In these last eight years the letters become more philosophical and tender, and reflect a new sense of mutual respect.

Unlike Jaspers, Arendt never confronted Heidegger directly about political questions and passed over his occasional remarks about politics without comment. She concentrated instead on Heidegger the philosopher, praising his interpretative genius ("no one reads or has ever read as you do") and his philosophical ambition ("by thinking the end of metaphysics and of philosophy you have made real room for thinking"). Professor Ettinger's reading of the late correspondence portrays Arendt as a slavish fool wasting her valuable time on the translation of his works and helping him to sell his manuscripts. Ettinger also mentions Arendt's 1969 tribute, "Martin Heidegger at Eighty," as proof that she was still so besotted that "she went to extraordinary pains to minimize and justify Heidegger's contribution to and support of the Third Reich." The notion that Hannah Arendt would justify anyone's Nazism is absurd. But it is true that she withheld reference to Heidegger's rectorship and later self-justifications until the end of her essay and placed it in a footnote. Which raises the legitimate question: Why?

Hannah Arendt often quoted an epigram of Rahel Varnhagen's, who once said of the conservative historian Friedrich von Gentz that "he seized upon untruth with the passion for truth." This is exactly how she had come to see Heidegger, whose intellectual passion she loved, but whose inability to distinguish obvious truth from obvious untruth she recognized only too well. She knew that Heidegger was politically dangerous but seemed to believe that his dangerousness was fueled by a passion that also inspired his philosophical thought. The problem of Heidegger was the problem of all great philosophers, nothing more, nothing less. Their thinking had to be cultivated and protected from the world, but they also must be kept from worldly political affairs, which are properly the concern of others—of citizens, of statesmen, of men of action.

Writing in 1969, forty-five years after first walking into his course on the *Sophist*, Arendt chose to remember above all what it was like to encounter a human being who lived for "passionate thinking," someone whose single-mindedness of purpose had left behind "something perfect." Without minimizing the significance of Heidegger's ghastly decision, she had come to see it as the result of a *déformation professionnelle*, an "attraction to the tyrannical" that has attended philosophy since its inception. In her unfinished study *The Life of the Mind* she was still meditating on this problem, trying to see if it might be solved by reestablishing distinctions among thinking, willing, and judging. Hannah Arendt was grappling with the problem of Heidegger until her dying day.

When Heidegger returned to teaching after his escapade as Nazi rector, one of his colleagues famously quipped, "Back from Syracuse?" The reference, of course, is to the three expeditions Plato made to Sicily in hopes of turning the young ruler Dionysius to philosophy and justice. The education failed, Dionysius remained a tyrant, and Plato barely escaped with his life. The parallel has been invoked more than once in discussions of Heidegger, the implication being that his tragicomic error was to have momentarily believed that philosophy could guide politics, especially the gutter politics of National Socialism. This possibility, too, Plato foresaw in his analysis of tyranny in the dialogues, especially the *Republic*.

One practical lesson that is often drawn from the *Republic* is that when philosophers try to become kings either their philosophy is corrupted, politics is corrupted, or both are. Therefore the only sensible thing is to separate them, leaving philosophers to cultivate their gardens with all the passion they have, but keeping them quarantined there so they can cause no harm. This is a political solution to the problem of philosophy and politics, and it is one Hannah Arendt advanced with some success in her American writings. This position permitted her to remain, in her own eyes, a genuine friend both of Heidegger's philosophy and of political decency.

Whether it is a defensible position is another matter. Traditionally, two sorts of objections, also inspired by Plato, have been made to the idea that philosophy and politics can be separated, one in the name of politics, the other in the name of philosophy. For those who care about political decency, the banishment of the tyrannically inclined is an attractive idea. But if philosophers take the rule of reason with them, what other standard will replace it? Who or what will stand against tyranny? This notorious question has been with us ever since the *Republic*, which documents the decline and fall of an imaginary city that has turned its back on philosophy. Hannah Arendt tried to address this danger in her own way, not altogether convincingly, by appealing at different times to tradition, statesmanship, civic virtue, and finally the faculty of "judgment" as hedges against tyranny.

A second objection has to do with the calling of philosophy itself. Plato's images of the love-mad philosopher seeking the beauty of Ideas, or of philosophical education as a painful climb out of a dark cave and into the sunlight, capture something of what drives the philosophical life but not necessarily how it is to be lived. As Plato describes him in the *Phaedrus* and the *Symposium*, the philosophical lover must be chaste and moderate if he is to sublimate his erotic drive and profit from it. Similarly, the myth of the cave in the *Republic* only ends once the philosopher is compelled to leave the sunlight and return to the cave to aid his fellows. Plato's lesson seems to be that, to be complete, philosophy must supplement its knowledge of Ideas with knowledge of the shadow realm of public life, where the passions and ignorance of human beings obscure the Ideas. And if philosophy is to illuminate that darkness, not add to it, it must begin by taming its own passions.

The most touching page in Karl Jaspers's *Notes on Martin Heidegger* is addressed to Heidegger directly. "I beseech you!" Jasper writes, "if ever we shared anything that can be called philosophical impulses, take responsibility for your own gift! Place it in the service of reason, of the reality of human worth and possibilities, instead of in the service of magic!" He felt betrayed by Heidegger as a human being, as a German, and as a friend, but especially as a philosopher. What he thought they shared in the early years of their friendship was the conviction that philosophy was a means of wresting one's existence from the grip of the commonplace and assuming responsibility for it. Then he saw a new tyrant enter his friend's soul, a wild passion that misled him into supporting the worst of political dictators and then enticed him into intellectual sorcery. In his unwillingness to leave Heidegger to his garden, Jaspers displayed more care for his former friend than Hannah Arendt did, and deeper love for the calling of philosophy. If nothing else, the Heidegger case had taught him a very Platonic lesson: in eros begin responsibilities.

Chapter II

CARL SCHMITT

CARL SCHMITT WAS born in the small Westphalian town of Plettenberg and died there in 1985 at the age of ninety-six. Virtually unknown in America, he is today considered in many European countries, especially in Germany, to be one of the most significant political theorists of the twentieth century. His books, the most important of which were written during the Weimar years, remain in print in many languages and are the subject of intense scholarly debate. Not even increased awareness of the circumstances surrounding Schmitt's active collaboration with the Nazi regime has dampened interest in the man and his writings.

The story of that collaboration is distressing. On May 1, 1933, while a professor of law at the University of Cologne, Schmitt applied to join the Nazi Party. Although he was hardly in the vanguard of the movement, as his party membership number (2,098,860) attests, his decision was not really surprising. During the previous decade he had become prominent as an antiliberal political and legal theorist, and as an outspoken critic of the Versailles Treaty and the Weimar

Constitution. As German parliamentary democracy disintegrated in the 1920s under the strains of political extremism on both left and right, Schmitt advocated temporary dictatorial rule by the Reich president, which he argued would be legal under the emergency powers granted by Article 48 of the Weimar Constitution.

When the German government finally invoked Article 48 in 1932 and appointed a Reich commissar for the state of Prussia in an attempt to stem the growing power of the Social Democrats, Schmitt defended the appointment before the State Constitutional Court. He lost the case, but his arguments in favor of emergency powers so impressed Nazi officials that after they came to power a few months later, they invited him to become one of the regime's legal counselors. Schmitt accepted, and within months newspapers were calling him the "crown jurist" of the Third Reich.

Like a number of other German intellectuals, including Martin Heidegger, Ernst Jünger, and Gottfried Benn, Schmitt publicly supported the Nazis in the early days of the Third Reich. But as Andreas Koenen shows in his detailed new book on the Schmitt "case," he went further than they did, becoming a committed, official advocate of the Nazi regime.[1] Under the patronage of Hermann Göring, he was appointed to the Prussian State Council, received a professorship in Berlin, and edited an important legal journal. The Nazis obviously hoped that Schmitt would supply juridical respectability

---

1. Andreas Koenen, *Der Fall Carl Schmitt: Sein Aufstieg zum "Kronjuristen" des Dritten Reiches* (Darmstadt: Wissenschaftliche Buchgesellschaft, 1995).

to Hitler's actions, and they were not disappointed. Soon after joining the party he wrote pamphlets defending the Führer principle, the priority of the Nazi Party, and racism, on the grounds that "all right is the right of a particular *Volk*." After the Night of the Long Knives in June 1934, when Hitler had Ernst Röhm and his other adversaries in the SA executed (among them a close friend of Schmitt's), Schmitt published an infamous and influential article arguing that Hitler's act "was itself the highest justice."

Schmitt reached the moral nadir of his collaboration in October 1936, when he spoke at a conference on "German Jurisprudence in the Struggle Against the Jewish Spirit."[2] There he called for purging Jewish works from libraries and encouraged his colleagues to avoid citing Jewish authors, or, when unavoidable, to identify them as Jews. "A Jewish author has for us no authority." After warning his colleagues that the Jews' renowned "logical sharpness" was only "a weapon aimed at us," he closed by quoting Hitler's words: "By warding off the Jews, I struggle for the work of the Lord."

In fact, Schmitt's speech was an effort to ward off his own enemies in the government at a time when the more radical and committed Nazis were purging those suspected of ideological softness. Like Heidegger during the same period, Schmitt found his classes under surveillance by the SS, and he was publicly attacked by

---

2. These remarks, for obvious reasons never reprinted, appear in the legal journal Schmitt edited: *Deutsche Juristen Zeitung*, October 15, 1936, pp. 1193–1199.

rival Nazi jurists. He made a last-ditch attempt to re-cover his influence between 1939 and 1941 by putting forward a theory of what he called the *Grossraum*, or geographical sphere of influence.[3] Although he appealed to the Monroe Doctrine as a precedent and claimed that the theory would preserve peace in an age of mass democracy and mechanized war, it was a trans-parent attempt to justify Hitler's imperialistic ambi-tions for the Third Reich. (Schmitt would later claim that he was trying to modify and redirect those ambi-tions.) But he failed to salvage his reputation within the regime, and as the war became total war he was almost completely forgotten. He lost most of his official posi-tions, but continued to teach in bombed-out Berlin until the war's end.

Schmitt's reputation as Hitler's "crown jurist" put him high on the list of suspects to be interrogated by the Allied forces occupying Berlin. He was arrested by the Russians, released, arrested again by the Americans, spent eighteen months in an internment camp, and was finally sent to Nuremberg for questioning. To his Russian interrogator he arrogantly announced, "I drank the Nazi bacillus but was not infected." In language reminiscent of Heidegger's self-justifications, Schmitt tried to persuade his American interrogator at Nurem-berg that he had felt superior to Hitler and had tried to impose his own interpretation of National Socialism.

---

3. Günther Maschke has edited a volume of Schmitt's articles on this theme: *Staat, Grossraum, Nomos: Arbeiten aus den Jahren 1916–1969* (Berlin: Duncker and Humblot, 1995).

As for the Holocaust, he reminded his questioner that "Christianity also ended in the murder of millions of people." In the end he was released and returned to his hometown, never to teach again.

53

Until his dying day Schmitt remained aggressively unrepentant about his collaboration. In the immediate postwar years he devoted much energy to writing self-exculpatory notebooks, some of which were published a few years ago in Germany under the title *Glossarium*, in a luxury edition with a gold placemarker and Schmitt's embossed signature on the cover.[4] The book created a sensation, shocking even Schmitt's defenders with the brutality of its language. "Jews remain Jews," Schmitt writes, "while Communists can improve themselves and change.... The real enemy is the assimilated Jew." "Better Hitler's enmity than the friendship of these returning émigrés and humanitarians." "What was really more indecent: joining Hitler in 1933, or spitting on him in 1945?" He even composed a short anti-Semitic poem, which can be loosely rendered:

> *Everyone speaks of elites,*
> *But the facts they refuse to face:*
> *there are only Isra-elites*
> *in a great planetary space.*

Schmitt bore his fate ignobly after the war, pouring his spleen into his lachrymose, self-pitying notebooks.

---

4. *Glossarium: Aufzeichnungen der Jahre 1947–1951*, edited by Eberhard Freiherr von Medem (Berlin: Duncker and Humblot, 1991).

But far from being forgotten, he became steadily more influential as time passed. Although he cultivated the myth of having retired into the "security of silence," he was in fact a tireless self-promoter who during the early years of the Federal Republic rained flattering letters and autographed books on anyone he thought might respond. A decade after he was interned by the Allies, Schmitt's home in Plettenberg became a pilgrimage site for any and all who wished to debate politics with the former "crown jurist."

Yet although Schmitt himself was undoubtedly a forceful personality, it was the rediscovery of his books that gradually established his current reputation in Europe. Raymond Aron, whose liberal convictions were unshakable, met with Schmitt and carried on an intermittent correspondence with him, and in his *Mémoires* called him a great social philosopher in the tradition of Max Weber. Alexandre Kojève, the Russian philosopher who gave lectures on Hegel attended by leading French intellectuals in Paris during the 1930s, visited Plettenberg in the Sixties, explaining to an acquaintance that "Schmitt is the only man in Germany worth talking to." Jacob Taubes, an influential and somewhat mysterious professor of Jewish theology in New York, Jerusalem, Paris, and Berlin, argued that the anti-Semitic Schmitt, along with Heidegger, was among the most important thinkers of our time. Taubes's advocacy was crucial in reintroducing Schmitt's work to German students when political radicalism was at its most popular during the Seventies; he thus encouraged one of the more curious phenomena of recent European intellectual history: left-wing Schmittism.[5]

In the decade since his death Schmitt has become the most intensely discussed political thinker in Germany. Hardly a month passes without a book about him or a new edition of his writings appearing there. Interest in Schmitt's life is also intense. Paul Noack's pedestrian biography has proved popular enough to warrant a paperback edition,[6] and there is even a regular publication called *Schmittiana* that collects newly discovered Schmitt correspondence, memoirs, bibliography, and gossip. Since Schmitt's political past is now widely known, this intense interest in him—which, to judge by the number of new translations and studies in English, is spreading—deserves examination.

The range of Carl Schmitt's political writings was vast and many of the most important works have yet to be translated. These include essays and books on the history of ideas, geopolitics, forms of government, the relation of church and state, and international relations, as well as an imposing treatise, *Constitutional*

---

5. Taubes defended his astonishing admiration for Schmitt in articles and lectures that have been published (posthumously) in *Ad Carl Schmitt: Gegenstrebige Fügung* (Berlin: Merve, 1987) and *Die Politische Theologie des Paulus* (Munich: Fink, 1993), pp. 132–141. A similar case of the attraction of opposites can be found in the pages of the American political journal *Telos*. Founded by left-wing students in 1968 as "An International Quarterly of Radical Theory," then after numerous mutations becoming "A Quarterly Journal of Post-Critical Thought," *Telos* turned its attention to Schmitt in the mid-Eighties and today publishes gurus of the European New Right such as Gianfranco Miglio and Alain de Benoist.

6. *Carl Schmitt: Eine Biographie* (Berlin: Propyläen, 1993).

Doctrine (1928), now in its eighth German edition, which is still considered a classic work on its subject.

Yet the best introduction to Schmitt's thought remains his *The Concept of the Political*, a short essay that Ernst Jünger once described as "a mine that silently explodes." It first appeared as a journal article in 1927, was expanded and revised several times by the author, and has now been reissued in English translation.[7] In it, Schmitt takes the question with which all political theory must begin—What is politics?—and reformulates it as: What is "the political" (*das Politische*)? By "the political" he does not mean a way of life or a set of institutions, he means a criterion for making a certain kind of decision. Morality finds such a criterion in the distinction between good and bad, aesthetics finds it in the distinction between beauty and ugliness. What is the criterion appropriate to politics? Schmitt answers in his characteristically oracular style: "The specific political distinction to which political actions and motives can be reduced is that between friend and enemy."

On the nature of friendship, a central theme in classical political thought, there is hardly a word to be found in all Schmitt's writings. We are left with the impression that friendship arises only from shared animosities. The enemy he means is a public enemy, not a private one; for Schmitt a collectivity is a political body only to the degree that it has enemies. If, as a German, I take France or Russia to be my enemy, I bear the individual

---

7. *The Concept of the Political*, translated by George Schwab (University of Chicago Press, 1996).

Frenchman or Russian no personal grudge, and his personal moral and aesthetic qualities are a matter of complete indifference to me. Enmity is a precisely defined relation that arises when, and only when, I recognize that certain persons or groups are "existentially something different and alien," and represent "the other, the stranger." Schmitt does not use the term "existential" casually; he believes that defining one's enemies is the first step toward defining one's inner self. "Tell me who your enemy is and I'll tell you who you are," he writes in his *Glossarium*; and again, more economically, "*Distinguo ergo sum.*"

If the act of distinguishing oneself from one's enemies is the essence of politics, then politics implies the hovering threat of conflict and, ultimately, the possibility of war. Thomas Hobbes was the first to see enmity developing naturally out of human relations, and his treatise *Leviathan* conceived a political order capable of controlling the outbreak of hostilities. Ever since Hobbes, political thinkers have associated war with the breakdown of healthy politics, treating it as an exception rather than the rule.

Schmitt, by contrast, believes that such exceptions show that *everything* is potentially political because everything—morals, religion, economics, art—can, in extreme cases, become a political issue, an encounter with an enemy, and be transformed into a source of conflict. Even the most liberal nations will beat their free-market plowshares into swords if they feel their survival genuinely to be at stake. Enmity simply is an essential element of human life: "The entire life of a human being is a struggle," he writes, "and every human being symbolically a combatant." A world without war would be a world without politics; a world without politics would be a world without enmity; and a world without enmity would be a world without human beings.

It is important to see here that Schmitt does not arrive at this view inductively after surveying the bloody record of political history. He is making an anthropological assumption about human nature that is meant to reveal the true lessons of history. If we accept this assumption, Schmitt thinks, we must then conclude that every human grouping requires a sovereign whose job it is to decide what to do in the extreme or exceptional case—most important of all, to engage in war or not, with one enemy or another. The state's sovereign decision is just that: a decision resting on no universal principle, and recognizing no natural bounds. (For Schmitt, the Roman practice of appointing temporary dictators to arbitrarily break the deadlock between competing social classes was the purest classical expression of the need for sovereign decision.)

This doctrine of Schmitt's has acquired the name "decisionism." Its target was modern liberalism, which conceives of the state as a neutral institution, under the rule of law, engaged in promoting compromises and resolving differences among individuals or groups. According to Schmitt, the liberal ideal of a morally universal and pacified world order developed in explicit opposition to the natural enmity between human groups and to the sovereign's arbitrary decision-making. Since it is not based on what Schmitt saw as the fundamental elements of the political, he claimed that there is "absolutely no liberal politics, only a liberal critique of politics."

This statement raises a conceptual difficulty that Schmitt was never able to resolve. At times he speaks as though liberalism had succeeded in overcoming natural enmity, and that this is to be regretted. He complains frequently that ours is an "age of neutralization and depoliticization," and that the healthy tensions of political life have been dissolved by private consumption, public entertainment, and "perpetual discussion"—all identified by him with liberalism. Yet he also asserts that liberalism is political, but unsuccessfully so. The weaknesses of liberal governments—their burdensome legal formalism, their hypocritical "neutrality," their oscillation between military pacifism and moral crusading—are the result of their attempts to evade the natural enmity that defines their own political existence. In either case, liberalism remains, in his view, contemptible.

Schmitt's voluminous pre-war writings on politics and jurisprudence, on which his current fame rests, can all be read as applications of the principles of political enmity and sovereign decisionism formulated in *The Concept of the Political*. In *Legality and Legitimacy* (1932) he maintained that the chaos of Weimar politics arose from liberals' unwillingness to confront their own domestic enemies on the extreme left and right. He criticized the Weimar Constitution for permitting parliamentary pluralism and the legal procedures that encouraged endless debate, without providing a way of maintaining the regime's unity and legitimacy. He also argued in *The Constitutional Guardian* (1931) that no individual or institution in Weimar was responsible for defending the constitution, and therefore the nation, against its internal enemies on the radical right and left. This view, it should be noted, was shared by many German jurists at the time.

The ultimate problem with liberalism, according to Schmitt, is that it fears decisions more than it fears enemies; but sovereign decisions are unavoidable in politics, even those founded on democratic principles. Having started from an assumption about belligerent human nature, Schmitt then tries to find historical evidence for the permanent political necessity of controlling it arbitrarily. His book *Dictatorship* (1921), a history of the institution from Roman times up to the Soviet "dictatorship of the proletariat," subtly tries to restore the conceptual legitimacy of dictatorship by asserting that the refusal to accept the necessity of moderate, temporary dictatorship had given birth to absolute ones. He followed this book with *The Intellectual Condition of Contemporary Parliamentarism* (1923), a very influential analysis in which he claimed that temporary dictatorships, which carry out the will of a united people immediately, are more consistent with democratic rule than liberal parliamentarism, which governs indirectly through procedures and elites.[8] Even his classic treatise *Constitutional Doctrine* depends on

---

8. While the German title of this work, *Die geistesgeschichtliche Lage des heutigen Parliamentarismus*, is virtually untranslatable in English, the title given to the MIT edition, *The Crisis of Parliamentary Democracy*, translated by Ellen Kennedy (1985), is quite misleading, since Schmitt's point is that "parliamentarism" is not democratic and therefore lacks legitimacy.

the assertion that constitutions are not "absolute," that they merely give concrete form to the distinctiveness of a *Volk* (a concept that remains disturbingly vague in Schmitt's writings); they therefore depend on a "previous political decision" giving that people "existence, integrity, and security."

Schmitt's postwar writings, while less polemical than his earlier ones, are if anything more ambitious. In *The Nomos of the Earth* (1950) he sketched out a mythical history of international relations based on the relation of human enmity to the conquest of land, sea, and air. Schmitt saw in the growing geographical ability of modern man to move and exert influence throughout the globe the cause of the simultaneous dissolution of sovereignty and the extension of enmity. The result of these tendencies in our century, he suggests, will be total wars, fought by countries against absolute enemies, using all their resources, and guided by universal but unenforceable moral principles. In his *Theory of the Partisan* (1963) Schmitt further speculated that the rise of guerrilla warfare and terrorism was linked to this same historical process, as wars between nations gave way to civil wars or wars of national liberation waged by supranational networks of partisans. While Schmitt clearly preferred the old system of spheres of influence ruled by enemy sovereigns conducting limited national wars (what he called a system of *Grossräume*), he expressed no nostalgia. His tone in his late works is cool and analytical.

Schmitt's influence owes a great deal to his direct, lapidary style, which is unencumbered by the peculiar burdens of German *Wissenschaft*. Compared to the baroque works of his academic contemporaries (and ours), his generally short books have a rare poetic quality. It is perhaps testimony to Schmitt's literary gift that he continues to be widely read today, despite public knowledge of his Nazism and anti-Semitism, and that so many in Germany continue to find him a source of instruction and even inspiration.

But there are more immediate reasons why Schmitt's political works are being studied today. One is that his political preoccupations—sovereignty, national unity, the dangers of ignoring enmity between nations, constitutional stability, war—have once again become the central themes of European politics. Another is that he is among the few political theorists concerned with such questions that Germany has seen in this century, and the only major one to be active after the war. The Federal Republic produced a number of important political historians, but political philosophy was dominated by Marxism and the Frankfurt School, which until recently tended to dismiss traditional political questions such as sovereignty, constitutionalism, and national self-assertion. In this vacuum, arguments have now been made, on both the left and the right, that Schmitt is the thinker from whom we have the most to learn about the problems of "the political."

The conservative case for studying Schmitt has been the most popular in the scholarly literature and the conservative German press, and has even influenced respected historians like Reinhart Koselleck and jurists like Ernst-Wolfgang Böckenförde. It presents itself publicly as a realistic corrective to liberalism rather than as an alternative to it. It takes from Schmitt the conviction that the ideas on which liberalism appears to be based—individualism, human rights, the rule of law—are fictions, and that the real foundations of national political life—unity, leadership, authority, arbitrary decisions—are illiberal. While the liberal fictions may be noble and even necessary for conducting the ordinary business of modern government, statesmen and political theorists must keep their eyes fixed on the real forces that drive politics. When they try to cultivate liberalism while neglecting the genuine foundations of a political order, the results are disastrous, especially in foreign policy. Ever since the two world wars, Western liberals have considered war "unthinkable." In the view of Schmitt's conservative admirers, this only means that war has become more thoughtless, not less frequent or less brutal. All liberal governments —Germany included—must be willing to help friends and harm enemies.

The left-wing case made for studying Schmitt is certainly a curiosity but also more interesting and radical than the conservative one. In the interviews with Schmitt published by the Maoist Joachim Schickel or in the recent books by the French writer Chantal Mouffe, there is a greater willingness to state opposition to liberalism openly in a spirit closer to Schmitt's own.[9] The

---

9. Joachim Schickel, *Gespräche mit Carl Schmitt* (Berlin: Merve, 1993) and Chantal Mouffe, editor, *The Return of the Political* (London: Verso, 1996).

left-wing writers, too, begin with his presupposition that liberal ideas are fictions; then they take the next step of arguing that such ideas are also the ideological weapons of a ruling class whose arbitrary decision established them in the public mind. Liberal "neutrality" (always in ironic quotes) actually serves the interests of particular classes and provides a structure for the forces of domination, aided by institutions, like schools and the press, and by repressive ideas, like toleration, that masquerade as liberation. In the view of some European leftists, Schmitt was a radical (if right-wing) democrat whose brutal realism can help us today to rediscover "the political" and restore a sense of legitimacy through the popular will. His critique of parliamentarism and the principle of neutrality can be seen in a left-wing light as unmasking domination in liberal societies; his unabashed defense of the friend–enemy distinction is said to remind us that politics is, above all, struggle.[10]

The transition from Herbert Marcuse to Carl Schmitt, in part by way of Michel Foucault's ideas about power and domination, proved remarkably easy for a small but important part of left-wing opinion in Germany,

---

10. In a 1982 article, Joschka Fischer, Germany's current foreign minister, explained the left's attraction to Schmitt in these terms: "During the student revolt both Ernst Jünger and Carl Schmitt were already considered within the SDS [Union of Socialist German Students] as a kind of intellectual 'hot tip,' surrounded by an aura of intellectual obscenity. They were fascists, obviously, but one still read them with great interest. The more militant the revolt became as the 'fighter' moved to center stage, the more obvious became the parallels."

France, and Italy, beginning in the Seventies. This was not a simple case of *les extrèmes se touchent*. Schmitt's antiliberalism provided a welcome substitute for Marxist economic and historical theories, which by then had fallen into disrepute. That Schmitt's later writings also discussed the end of colonialism, the rise of guerrilla war, and the dangers of economic globalization only made him more attractive to freethinking elements of the European left. Little wonder, then, that young revolutionaries who had once cut sugarcane in Cuba found themselves taking the train to Plettenberg, sharing compartments with their conservative adversaries.

To judge by most recent accounts of Schmitt's thought, then, Schmitt was (depending on one's leanings) either a classical political theorist who studied the foundations of politics without liberal moral illusions, or a radical exposer of liberal hypocrisy and ideology. But such views of his intellectual legacy hardly do justice to Schmitt's deeper ambitions, which were not those of a mere commentator on contemporary politics. There is a remarkable lack of seriousness among those studying and promoting Schmitt today, whatever their partisan motivations, an unwillingness to probe too deeply into his moral universe. For even if we leave aside how Schmitt applied his doctrines to the political circumstances of his time, we are still left wondering what the basis of those doctrines really was. What convinces Schmitt that human enmity is existentially so fundamental? Why is he so determined to portray the political order as resting entirely on the arbitrary decision of a sometimes hidden sovereign? What makes liberal society so contemptible in his eyes? Schmitt himself argues for his views by claiming to reduce political phenomena to their basic principles. It is therefore only appropriate that we seek out his own deeper assumptions and motivations.

The first critic to begin such an examination of Schmitt's work was Leo Strauss, the German-Jewish political philosopher who later had a distinguished career at the University of Chicago. In 1932 Strauss, then a young man, published a review of *The Concept of the Political* which Schmitt thought the most penetrating thing written about his essay.[11] At the time Strauss shared many of Schmitt's views about the failures of modern liberalism, but he also noted the equivocations in Schmitt's case against it. Hobbes assumed man's natural belligerency in order to make the case for controlling it. Schmitt, for his part, argued against liberalism's attempts to control human enmity, which he saw as natural and necessary, and which he gave every indication of wishing to intensify. Strauss perceived that Schmitt was not just lecturing utopian liberals about an inescapable "logic of the political"; he was actually an admirer of "animal power" who was advocating political enmity and decisionism. In Strauss's words, Schmitt's polemic was meant "to clear the field

11. This review is reprinted in the English translation of *The Concept of the Political* and in Heinrich Meier's *Carl Schmitt and Leo Strauss*, discussed below. Schmitt was so taken with Strauss's criticism that he recommended the latter for a Rockefeller grant to conduct research abroad, a recommendation that, as fate would have it, spared Strauss from the events that soon followed in Germany.

for the battle of decision" between the liberal faith and "the opposite spirit and faith, which, as it seems, still has no name."

Strauss cast doubt on Schmitt's carefully contrived image as a political realist but did not speculate further about the content of this nameless faith. That task has now been undertaken by Heinrich Meier, a diligent German scholar who in 1988 wrote a densely argued book asserting that Schmitt recognized the force of Strauss's criticisms and substantially changed later editions of *The Concept of the Political* in light of them. Meier's detective work, which has now appeared in English translation as *Carl Schmitt and Leo Strauss: The Hidden Dialogue*, made a case for seeing Schmitt primarily as a "political theologian," whose ambitions had been exposed by the "political philosopher" Strauss.[12]

Though Schmitt had indeed published a short work with the title *Political Theology* in 1922, many specialists in Schmitt's work considered Meier's thesis to be forced and idiosyncratic, and I once shared this view myself. Yet when Schmitt's *Glossarium* appeared in 1991 and German readers discovered bizarre theological reflections on nearly every page, Meier's book received unexpected confirmation. Since then much Schmitt scholarship has concentrated on the theological aspects of his thought. Some of this work, as we see in the volume edited by Bernd Wacker, usefully connects Schmitt with the general crisis in German theology and political

12. Heinrich Meier, *Carl Schmitt and Leo Strauss: The Hidden Dialogue* (University of Chicago Press, 1995).

thought at the beginning of the century, particularly with Protestant and Catholic thinkers such as Karl Barth, Friedrich Gogarten, and Erik Peterson. Much of it, like Günter Meuter's bloated and unfocused book on Schmitt's "fundamentalist critique of the age," simply muddies the issues.[13]

Standing far above the rest, however, is Heinrich Meier's new study, *The Lesson of Carl Schmitt*, which covers all of Schmitt's writings, including his *Glossarium*.[14] It shows Meier to be a theologically "musical" reader of Schmitt (Walter Benjamin was another) who hears the deep religious chords sounding beneath the surface of his seductive prose. Meier's work has forced everyone to take a second look at the assumptions underlying Schmitt's better-known writings and reconsider some that have been ignored.

One of Schmitt's half-forgotten but explicitly theological works is his early *Roman Catholicism and Political Form* (1923), which has now appeared in a new English translation.[15] This work is important be-

---

13. Bernd Wacker, editor, *Die eigentlich katholische Verschärfung: Konfession, Theologie und Politik im Werk Carl Schmitts* (Munich: Fink, 1994); Günter Meuter, *Der Katechon: Zu Carl Schmitts fundamentalistischer Kritik der Zeit* (Berlin: Duncker und Humblot, 1994). See also, more recently, Ruth Groh, *Arbeit an der Heillosigkeit der Welt: Zur politisch-theologischen Mythologie und Anthropologie Carl Schmitts* (Frankfurt: Suhrkamp, 1998).

14. Heinrich Meier, *The Lesson of Carl Schmitt: Four Chapters on the Distinction between Political Theology and Political Philosophy* (University of Chicago Press, 1998).

15. *Roman Catholicism and Political Form*, translated by G. L. Ulmen (Greenwood Press, 1996).

cause it shows that beneath Schmitt's surface realism lie some very firm notions about the ideal political order and how nearly the Catholic Church once embodied it. The great political virtue of the Church, he writes, is always to have understood itself as a *complexio oppositorum*, a complex of doctrinal and social opposites brought into harmonic unity. The Church places the need for unity above all else since it must rule authoritatively over the society and represent it before God. Extending the ideas of Max Weber, to whom he was deeply indebted, Schmitt argued that the Church's authority is legitimized symbolically through ritual rather than legally through neutral rules; it sees itself as representing the entire body of the faithful, not particular individuals. Schmitt saw the Church's understanding of the good political order as having come under attack in the modern age, threatened by the idea of political individualism and by a capitalist economy that subordinated social ends to calculating means. While he was under no illusion about the Church's reacquiring political authority in modern Europe, he had a very precise (if fictional) idea of the unified Christian world we had lost, and this remained his standard for measuring all subsequent political developments.

This is not to say that Schmitt was a Catholic thinker in any traditional sense. Although he was born into a conservative Catholic family, his theological speculations are an entirely homemade brew of modern existentialism and premodern heresies that the Church suppressed centuries ago. Schmitt's God is not the God of Saint Thomas, ruling over a rationally ordered natural world in which human beings find their place, but a hidden, decision-making God, a sovereign who has already revealed divine truths once and for all, and whose authority offers the sole foundation for those truths. And the central truth He has revealed to us is that everything is a matter of divine politics. In his short and powerful essay *Political Theology* (1922) Schmitt writes:

> The political is the total, and as a result we know that any decision about whether something is *unpolitical* is always a *political* decision.... This also holds for the question whether a particular theology is a political or an unpolitical theology.

As Heinrich Meier explains, this equation of politics and theology is for Schmitt a revealed truth closed to the rational inquiry of secular philosophy, which cannot hope to penetrate the mystery of revelation. At a certain point, one must simply decide—about politics as much as about faith. The sovereign decides on political action and we must decide the question "Christ or Barabbas?" The problem with liberals, Schmitt remarks ironically, is that they meet this question with a proposal to adjourn or appoint a committee of inquiry.

If Schmitt's decisionism is difficult to explain in orthodox theological categories, his principle of political enmity is impossible to reconcile with his professed Christianity. Although he appeals to the doctrine of original sin, writing that "all genuine political theories presuppose man to be evil," his distinction between friend and enemy is closer to the gnostic bloodlust of Joseph de Maistre than to the Sermon on the Mount. In several places he speaks of the creation of the world as issuing from a divine struggle, and human conflict for him seems to be a reenactment of this struggle, willed by a God who has condemned us to be political. Cain was set against Abel, Esau against Jacob, and the whole of humanity was set against Satan, whom God told, "I will put enmity between thee and the woman, and between thy seed and her seed" (Genesis 3:15). In *The Concept of the Political* Schmitt finds the true character of human political enmity captured in a speech by Oliver Cromwell, who once described papist Spain as "the natural enemy, the providential enemy [whose] enmity is put into him by God." Commenting on this passage, Meier remarks that Schmitt seemed to believe "that the enemy is part of a divine order, and that war has the character of a divine judgment."

Seen in this light, the liberal search for peace and security represents a rebellion against God; and the serpent who tempted us was none other than Thomas Hobbes. Schmitt, who is sometimes mistaken for a Hobbesian, actually wrote a critical study of him, *The Leviathan in the State Theory of Thomas Hobbes* (1938), which has now appeared in English.[16] This is perhaps Schmitt's most self-revealing and (not by chance) most anti-Semitic work, and Meier is right to concentrate on

---

16. *The Leviathan in the State Theory of Thomas Hobbes: Meaning and Failure of a Political Symbol*, translated by George Schwab and Erna Hilfstein (Greenwood Press, 1996).

it. Like Schmitt, Hobbes understood man to be belligerent and religion to be simultaneously a source of political unity and conflict. But rather than accept perpetual
conflict as the price to be paid for the unity offered by a
Christian polity, Hobbes, in Schmitt's analysis, devised
an absolutely secular polity ruled mechanistically by
a "mortal God" who was the central controlling force
in a civil—that is, non-Christian—religion. By replacing the true God with a human one, Schmitt alleges,
Hobbes taught Christian Europe how to evade God's
divine command, "fight thy enemy."

In Schmitt's reasoning, the real beneficiaries of modern liberal peace were not cowards and atheists but
Jews, the quintessential domestic "strangers." We learn
this, he says, by studying Spinoza, "the first liberal Jew,"
who, following Hobbes, preached toleration of private
religious beliefs. This principle enticed Christians into
letting down their guard and permitting Jews to pursue
their "will to power" through Masonic Lodges, syna-
gogues, and literary circles, which in turn spawned the
political and economic order dominated by Jews today.
According to an ancient kabbalistic tradition, Schmitt
asserts, the Jews stand on the sidelines while the Christian peoples heed God's call to battle, and the Jews
"then eat the flesh of those killed and live off it."
Liberalism simply institutionalizes this practice.[17]

The liberal secular state, then, is the product of a
battle not between nations or classes, but between man

---

17. Schmitt's relation to "the Jewish Question" is the subject of Rafael Gross's
comprehensive study, *Carl Schmitt und die Juden* (Frankfurt: Suhrkamp, 2000).

and God. Man decided that the enmity between human beings that God commanded was too harsh; he preferred peace and plenty to the miracles of saints and the decisions of sovereign rulers. The prototypical figure of the modern age is the Romantic, a new human type whom Schmitt acutely dissected in *Political Romanticism* (1919). Freed from God and rulers, cushioned by the comforts of bourgeois life, the Romantic is an empty shell of a man who flits from commitment to commitment as occasion demands, conversant with all faiths but believing in none.

Against the Romantic with his tolerant liberalism stands an assortment of modern revolutionaries and reactionaries who continue to see political struggles in the apocalyptic terms of religious war. The anarchist Bakunin's motto, "*Ni Dieu, ni maître,*" earned him Schmitt's respect as the "theologian of the anti-theological, the dictator of the anti-dictatorial," while the nineteenth-century Catholic counterrevolutionary Donoso Cortés is praised by Schmitt for perceiving the satanic quality in man's rebellion. Enemies in the great conflicts of the revolutions of 1848, these two precisely understood each other; they saw the decisions before them and made them without flinching.

Those who call for "existential" decisions always manage to be living in decisive times. As Meier shows in the fine concluding chapter of his study, Schmitt saw his work as a bulwark against the forces of modern history, which in his view had reached a crisis. "I am a theologian of jurisprudence," he writes in his *Glossarium*. He was, he wrote, devoted to "a real Catholic intensification (against the neutralizers, the aesthetic decadents, against the abortionists, corpse burners, and pacifists)." The Jews were not random targets of Schmitt's wrath; nor was his anti-Semitism calculated merely to curry favor with Nazi officials.[18] In his demonology, Jews represented the "providential" enemy who must be resisted by doing "the work of the Lord."

That Schmitt never considered his decision to support the Nazis to have been more than a tactical error is also entirely consistent with his political theology. His romanticizing of Catholic institutions, his praise of Mussolini, his attempts to salvage democratic legitimacy from the legalism of the Weimar system, and his work for Hitler, while not consistent, reflect a willingness to encourage any force that might do battle against the secularized liberal age. He describes himself repeatedly as a *katechon*, the Greek term Saint Paul

---

18. George Schwab, Schmitt's first American promoter, continues to maintain a "strategic" interpretation of Schmitt's most outrageous anti-Semitic statements, as we learn in his preface to the new translation of *The Leviathan in the State Theory of Thomas Hobbes*. While recognizing that Schmitt clearly indicts the Jews for exploiting Hobbes's theory, Schwab insists that the much-persecuted Schmitt had "neutralized" the "venom" he reserved for them in his infamous speech at the 1936 Juristentag by now including Catholics, Presbyterians, and Freemasons in his attack; he then remarks that the book is "remarkably free of Nazi jargon" (pp. xx–xxi).

To make matters worse, Schwab then naively reports Schmitt's later comment to him that the Jewish problem had been solved now that "at last they [Jews] again have contact with a soil they can call their own"—as if this staple of postwar anti-Semitism was simply another facet of Schmitt's long-held views on liberal jurisprudence. Fortunately, the English translation of this work is truthful to the German original and permits the critical reader to understand Schmitt on this issue the way he understood himself.

uses when speaking of the force that holds off the Anti-Christ until the Second Coming (2 Thessalonians 2:6). As for his speculations about the new "*nomos* of the earth," they reflect nothing so much as the messianic longings of an aging apocalyptic thinker.

75

Heinrich Meier's treatment of Schmitt's writings is morally analytical without moralizing, a remarkable feat in view of Schmitt's past. He wishes to understand what Schmitt was after rather than to dismiss him out of hand or bowdlerize his thought for contemporary political purposes. And if this seriousness leads Meier to overstate vastly Schmitt's own significance as a thinker, it has the advantage of throwing indirect light on an important phenomenon that he represents within liberal society.

Like any other political doctrine, liberalism makes assumptions about things human and divine, and these assumptions are, and ought to remain, open to disinterested reflection. Those who seriously question such assumptions are not wrong to do so and their arguments must be engaged. But for nearly two centuries now, the advocates of liberal ideas have also found themselves confronted by opponents like Schmitt, who are so convinced that the modern age represents a cosmic mistake that they are willing to consider any extreme, intellectual or political, to correct it. While few of Schmitt's contemporary promoters may share his peculiar theological vision, many display his violent distaste for liberal society; and like him they long passionately for a new dispensation. Given the power of such passions, and the damage they can cause, we should be scrupulous in distinguishing liberalism's genuinely philosophical critics from those who practice the politics of theological despair. Anyone who tries to learn from Carl Schmitt without making this elementary distinction will have learned nothing at all.

Chapter III

WALTER BENJAMIN

IN 1968 HANNAH ARENDT edited *Illuminations*, the first collection of essays by Walter Benjamin to appear in English. At that time little was known about Benjamin outside Germany, except that he was a talented and idiosyncratic literary critic who had committed suicide while fleeing the Nazis in 1940. The essays Arendt selected for *Illuminations* primarily reflected his literary achievements, among them dense ruminations on Kafka, Baudelaire, Proust, Brecht, and Leskov, as well as a charming essay on book collecting. Only the last two essays, on the mechanical reproduction of artworks and on the philosophy of history, give any clue to Benjamin's more profound philosophical ambitions.

In Germany, however, a bitter debate was already raging over those ambitions when *Illuminations* appeared. Theodor Adorno and his wife, Gretel, had edited the first German collection of Benjamin's selected writings in the mid-Fifties. This two-volume set was intended to secure Benjamin's place in the pantheon of the Frankfurt School, which had supported and published him in the 1930s. In the Sixties, however, the Adornos came under strong, generally unscrupulous, attack by members of the German New Left, who charged them with bowdlerizing Benjamin's revolutionary Marxism. This political dispute was only intensified with the publication in 1966 of Benjamin's selected correspondence, edited jointly by Theodor Adorno and the Jewish historian Gershom Scholem, one of Benjamin's oldest friends. These letters showed that although Benjamin professed to be a Marxist of sorts from the mid-Twenties on, from his first days to his last he was profoundly absorbed by theological questions. This aspect of his thought appears most clearly in his exchanges with Scholem, which make up the largest surviving portion of his correspondence. What began in Germany as a narrow squabble over Benjamin's legacy soon became a significant controversy over the relation between political and theological ideas.

In 1994 an edition of these selected letters was translated and published as *The Correspondence of Walter Benjamin, 1910–1940*.[1] Although from a purely editorial standpoint this volume left much to be desired, it nonetheless gave the English reader a window into an important—indeed decisive—aspect of Benjamin's thought. The conventional view of Benjamin in the Anglo-American world is that he managed where oth-

---

1. *The Correspondence of Walter Benjamin, 1910–1940*, edited and annotated by Gershom Scholem and Theodor W. Adorno, translated by Manfred Jacobson and Evelyn Jacobson (University of Chicago Press, 1994). The problems with this edition are many, beginning with the fact that owing to contractual constraints the University of Chicago Press was unable to add any critical apparatus, leaving readers in the dark about many oblique references

ers failed to marry a congenial Marxism with insightful and imaginative criticism, offering an example for others to follow. What the letters instead show is a more theologically inspired and politically unstable thinker, one whose messianic yearnings drew him dangerously near the flames of political passion that engulfed Europe for much of the last century.

Walter Benjamin was born into a well-off family of Berlin Jews in 1892. His father had made a modest fortune as an auctioneer and art dealer, and later expanded it as an investor. Benjamin wrote two memoirs of his youth, "A Berlin Chronicle" and "Berlin Childhood," bittersweet reflections on his privileged upbringing in the well-to-do western section of the city, filled with memories of promenades, cool relations with his parents, and absurd luxury. Because young Walter was

---

made by the correspondents. Then, for reasons of its own, the Press chose to offer little information about the book's relation to the German original, and some of that is incorrect. A short "Note on Sources" makes the strange claim that, while the original edition was copyrighted in 1966, it "was published only in 1978." (In fact, the German original book was published in 1966; the 1978 edition was a revised one.) It then notes that 33 of the 332 letters were originally translated in *The Correspondence of Walter Benjamin and Gershom Scholem, 1932–1940* (Schocken, 1989), without further elaboration. That important volume, however, is the translation of a 1980 German collection that includes a great number of Scholem's own letters to Benjamin, which were miraculously preserved in an East German archive and only released in 1977. The relation between the Chicago volume and these four other volumes—the two German editions of the Benjamin letters, and the German and English editions of the Scholem–Benjamin correspondence from 1932 to 1940—is left utterly obscure. Nor do we learn that new editions of Benjamin's letters are currently being prepared in Germany, one of which has now appeared in English translation: *Theodor Adorno and Walter Benjamin, The Complete Correspondence, 1928–1940* (Harvard University Press, 1999).

somewhat sickly as a boy, his parents sent him away for two years to a provincial boarding school, one of whose directors, Gustav Wyneken, was a major force in the German Youth Movement. Benjamin soon began writing for one of the movement's journals, *Der Anfang*, and remained allied with Wyneken and his Nietzschean pedagogical movement until the First World War.

Benjamin's early correspondence contains much discussion of the Youth Movement, though one also witnesses his growing awareness of his status as a Jew in Germany. We know little about the Benjamin family's attitude toward Judaism except that they were liberal without being entirely assimilated. We learn here that young Walter, like many German Jews drawn to the early essays of Martin Buber, flirted with political Zionism in the summer of 1912. But in a letter to his friend Ludwig Strauss later that September, he wrote: "I see three Zionist forms of Jewishness: Palestine Zionism (a natural necessity); German Zionism in its halfness; and cultural Zionism, which sees Jewish values *everywhere* and works for them. Here I will stay, and I believe I must stay." This would remain his position throughout his life.[2]

Benjamin's attitude toward political Zionism reflected a more fundamental inclination to escape the ugly political atmosphere of the period. Among the surprises

---

2. This letter, not included in the English edition and only incompletely in the *Gesammelte Schriften*, is translated from the original copy in Jerusalem by Anson Rabinbach in his "Between Enlightenment and Apocalypse: Benjamin, Bloch and Modern German Messianism," *New German Critique* (Winter 1985), p. 96.

contained in these letters is the utter absence of political commentary as the First World War began, and
its meagerness for some years thereafter. Benjamin
first appears to us as an "unpolitical man"—if not
quite like Thomas Mann, then like so many others
of his generation who abandoned the faltering institutions of bourgeois Europe in order to explore aesthetic experience and irrationalist "philosophies of
life" (*Lebensphilosophien*).

Nonetheless, despite Benjamin's attempts to ignore
the war, it intruded from every side. In August 1914,
in despair over the coming catastrophe, two of his
closest friends committed suicide together in the apart-
ment where his Berlin circle often gathered, and not
long afterward Wyneken published a nationalistic
manifesto, "Youth and War," that provoked Benjamin
to dissociate himself from his former teacher and the
Youth Movement. He obtained an exemption from
military service in 1917 by faking an attack of sciatica,
and by that summer was in voluntary exile in Switzerland with his wife, Dora, whom he had married that
April. His new friend Gershom Scholem, who obtained
an exemption by feigning mental illness, arrived in
Bern in 1918, and they began the intense intellectual
exchange that would prove so fruitful for both men.

Scholem and Benjamin had first met in 1915, though
Scholem remembered seeing Benjamin participate in a
public debate on Zionism two years earlier. As Scholem
recounted in his two memoirs, he and the older Benjamin were immediately drawn to each other, despite
philosophical and religious differences. Scholem, too,

had grown up in the bosom of Berlin liberal Judaism but as a young man grew appalled by its cultural compromises. When he received a picture of Theodor Herzl as a Christmas present one year, he was so disgusted that he began to learn Hebrew, mastering it quickly. By 1917 his family had turned him out of the house for becoming a Zionist, and he had decided to study the history of Kabbala.

Benjamin did not share this passion and did not even know Hebrew. But Scholem sensed in Benjamin a "devotion to the spiritual like that of a scribe cast out into another world, who has set off in search of his 'scripture.' "[3] The more Scholem studied the traditions of Jewish mysticism and messianism, the more he came to see Benjamin as "a theologian marooned in the realm of the profane."[4]

The publication in Germany of Benjamin's correspondence drew attention for the first time to his early philosophical writings, with their strong theological overtones. Read along with the letters of the period, they largely confirm Scholem's instinct about the spiritual temperament of his friend. One of the earliest of his writings to survive is a short, unpublished manuscript of 1917–1918 entitled "On the Program of the Coming Philosophy." Both Benjamin and Scholem had begun their philosophical studies by reading Kant, whose work had recently been revived at the University

3. Gershom Scholem, *Walter Benjamin: The Story of a Friendship* (Jewish Publication Society of America, 1981), p. 53.

4. Gershom Scholem, *On Jews and Judaism in Crisis* (Schocken, 1976), p. 187.

of Marburg. Like the early Romantics, they were simultaneously attracted and repelled by Kant's rigorous distinction between the phenomenal world open to science and the noumenal world of moral ends; they were attracted by the recognition of a metaphysical realm beyond the material, repelled by the needle's eye that Kant placed between the two. Benjamin took it as a philosophical challenge to overcome Kant's distinction within the frame of Kant's own thought, calling this "the central task of the coming philosophy." What philosophy needs, he writes, is the "epistemological foundation of a higher concept of experience," which will make "religious experience logically possible." This theological conception of experience is echoed in a 1918 letter to Scholem, in which Benjamin states that all ethics need a foundation in metaphysics, in order to understand "the absolute divine context of order, whose highest sphere is doctrine and whose embodiment and first cause is God."

Statements like these, expressing a vague desire to re-affirm religious experience in the wake of the Enlightenment, are commonplaces in the history of philosophical Romanticism. And, more often than not, they are allied with a crypto-theological view of language, which Benjamin shared with his eighteenth- and nineteenth-century predecessors Hamann, Jacobi, Schleiermacher, Novalis, and Friedrich Schlegel. In 1916 he wrote to Martin Buber:

> Every action that derives from the expansive tendency to string words together seems terrible to

me. . . . I can understand writing as such as poetic, prophetic, objective in terms of its effect, but in any case only as magical, that is as un-mediated.

To Hugo von Hofmannsthal he later remarked that "every truth has its home, its ancestral palace, in language."

Benjamin attempted to elaborate these intuitions about language and truth in a difficult essay, "On Language as Such and on the Language of Man" (1916). Here he rejects the "bourgeois" view that language is based on conventions in favor of the "mystical" view that names are divine essences, which had become obscured and confused after Babel. Benjamin, however, insists that by translating human languages into one another, men can begin to reconstruct the "nameless, unspoken" language of nature, which is a "residue of the creative word of God" and out of which "the ultimate clarity of the word of God unfolds."

Benjamin was aware that he was treading on the Romantics' path, and over the next few years set out to confront them directly. He did so in his first scholarly dissertation and only traditionally academic book, The *Concept of Art Criticism in German Romanticism*, which was accepted by the faculty at Bern in 1919. In it he argues that criticism can be so powerful that it becomes more valuable than artistic creation itself. The nineteenth-century Romantics valued criticism because they idealized the poet, the writer, the painter; Benjamin idealizes the critic as a conjurer teasing truths out of the objects in which they have been sealed.

"Through Kant's philosophical works," he writes, "the concept of criticism took on an almost magical meaning for the younger generation.... To be critical meant to raise thought so far above all constraint that, through the perception of the falseness of constraints, knowledge of the truth takes flight as if by magic."[5]

This view would have the most far-reaching consequences for Benjamin's career. He develops it further in his famous essay on Goethe's *Elective Affinities*, which begins with the bold claim that what the reader holds in his hands is not "commentary" but criticism, which "seeks the truth content of a work of art." This task is then given a mystical formulation:

> If, to use a simile, one views the growing work as a burning funeral pyre, then the commentator stands before it like a chemist, the critic like an alchemist. Where for the former, wood and ash remain the sole objects of his analysis, for the latter only the flame itself preserves an enigma: that of what is alive. Thus the critic inquires into the truth, whose living flame continues to burn over the heavy logs of the past and the light ashes of experience.

For Benjamin, then still in his late twenties, this invocation of alchemy may have been no more than a simile, but his friend Scholem took such statements

---

5. "Der Begriff der Kunstkritik in der deutschen Romantik," *Gesammelte Schriften*, Vol. I.1 (Frankfurt: Suhrkamp, 1972–1989), p. 51.

very seriously. Scholem shared Benjamin's dissatisfaction with Kant and with the denatured "liberal" theology that grew up in his wake; Scholem, too, found the bourgeois pieties of Wilhelmine culture empty and stifling. But rather than turn to Romanticism, he began to study the mystical kabbalistic texts of medieval Judaism, from which he hoped to gain historical perspective on the spiritual dissatisfactions with "debased" experience, to learn how they arose in the history of religion, and to understand the reactions to them. This is the light in which he began to see Benjamin's early writings—and it is a clarifying light.

Scholem's research taught him that Judaism had always experienced a tension between the discipline of the law, which was a preparation for redemption, and a powerful messianic impulse, which regularly strained against such discipline and sought immediate, direct contact with the divine. This impulse was antinomian, apocalyptic, and utopian. It rejected any simple appeal to tradition or historical progress, believing instead in "transcendence breaking in upon history, an intrusion in which history itself perishes, transformed into ruins because it is struck by a beam of light shining into it from an outside source." Traditionally, Jewish orthodoxy had tried to stifle this impulse, going so far as to deny or distort its history. But all such efforts were doomed because "the power of redemption seems to be built into the clockwork of life lived in the light of revelation." The "anarchic breeze" of messianism was destined to blow through the house of orthodoxy whenever the living sources of religion had been relegated to the cellar. "It is a profound truth," Scholem writes, "that a well-ordered house is a dangerous thing."[6]

In his view, German Judaism of the early twentieth century was one such house. Hermann Cohen, the leading figure of the neo-Kantian philosophical school, was the most prominent proponent of reinterpreting Judaism as an ethical system, which he undertook in works such as *The Religion of Reason Out of the Sources of Judaism* (1929). In his other writings Cohen asserted that Jews and Germans could exist harmoniously in a liberal society, which he considered Germany to be. Against this consensus an entire generation of young Jewish thinkers would rebel, some before World War I, others just after. Scholem and Benjamin belonged to this generation, as did Martin Buber, Franz Rosenzweig, Franz Kafka, Ernst Bloch, and Leo Strauss. In their letters, Scholem and Benjamin seem very conscious of their affinities with these writers, and they discuss them frequently. Both were particularly taken with Rosenzweig's *Star of Redemption* (1921), which they considered a significant critique of both Kantianism and liberal Judaism, and with the stories of Kafka, which offered, as Scholem later put it, "an intuitive affirmation of mystical themes which walk a fine line between religion and nihilism."[7]

This "fine line" is the kabbalistic line, and the more Scholem followed it in Jewish history, the more he

---

6. *The Messianic Idea in Judaism* (Schocken, 1971), pp. 10, 321, 21.

7. Unpublished letter of 1937, translated in David Biale, *Gershom Scholem: Kabbalah and Counter-History* (Harvard University Press, second edition, 1982), p. 31.

believed he could trace its path through his generation of Jewish youth seeking redemption in a profane world. Within this generation, no figure attracted and perplexed him more than Benjamin. Beneath Benjamin's complaints about the poverty of modern experience or the coldness of reason, beneath his vitalistic celebrations of art and language, Scholem heard the age-old voice of those called "masters of a holy soul" in kabbalistic lore. Such souls were blessed with great powers of perception and were capable of reviving desiccated religious cultures. But, as Scholem also knew, they were equally vulnerable to illusion and self-destruction—especially under modern secular conditions, and especially when they turned to politics.

Benjamin's interest in political questions began to develop only in the Twenties, after the war and just as his private life was beginning to unravel. In 1920 economic conditions in Germany forced his return from Switzerland, and once in Berlin he fell out with his parents, who were putting pressure on him to find a regular job. To complicate matters further, in 1921 both Benjamin and his wife, Dora, fell in love with other people —she with Walter's old schoolmate Ernst Schoen, he with the sculptress Jula Cohn, the sister of another friend. A temporary separation was agreed upon, then a reconciliation for the sake of their young son. Neither affair lasted, but the marriage was shattered and the couple finally divorced in 1930.

Although the outward shape of Benjamin's life changed dramatically during this trying period, his first political writings show remarkable continuity with the theological speculations of his Swiss years. In 1920 he published "The Critique of Violence," a dense and not altogether successful essay on Georges Sorel's *Réflexions sur la violence*, which was becoming a key text for thinkers on the radical right and left. Benjamin criticizes Sorel, but he shares Sorel's view that bourgeois life and parliamentary politics are based on an illegitimate official violence, and he proposes that a different kind of violence—a regenerative, "law-making" violence—can bring about a new social order. Less explicit about violence, but no less apocalyptic, is the short "Theologico-Political Fragment" written later that year. Here Benjamin writes that although "only the Messiah himself consummates all history," history does not prepare for his arrival: the messianic moment comes unannounced, bringing history to an abrupt, perhaps violent stop. To strive for the passing away of the natural world is, Benjamin says here, "the task of world politics, whose method must be called nihilism."

If Benjamin had never written another word about politics after these essays, we would probably understand him today as a proponent of that diffuse strain of vitalism in early-twentieth-century Continental thought that drew many intellectuals to radical right-wing views and movements after World War I. As a young man Benjamin had sought out Ludwig Klages, the popular (and later anti-Semitic) philosopher whose magnum opus, *The Mind as Adversary of the Soul* (1929–1932), attacks the rationalistic tradition of Western philosophy for distorting the vitalistic sources of knowledge, will, and aesthetic experience. Benjamin also carefully studied and wrote on the works of Johann Jakob Bachofen, the nineteenth-century ethnologist whose theories of pagan myth and symbols had recently been promoted by the Stefan George circle, of which Klages was an early member. Benjamin's correspondence shows that throughout his life he was fascinated with these right-wing theorists of myth, eroticism, power, dreams, and imagination—though it must be added that he was always repelled by their politics once he understood them.

Benjamin's notion of criticism as alchemy, his conviction that politics is a matter of apocalyptic nihilism, and his fascination with right-wing vitalism all came together in his major work of the Twenties, *Ursprung des deutschen Trauerspiels* (The Origin of German Tragic Drama).[8] Benjamin had moved to Frankfurt in 1923 to pursue the advanced degree that would have permitted him to teach in a university and to be recognized, as he later put it, as "the foremost critic of German literature." It was a disastrous decision from nearly every standpoint. His professors were hostile to his planned dissertation on the long-neglected German "sorrow-plays" (*Trauerspiele*) of the seventeenth century, which they considered an idiosyncratic subject. Moreover, Benjamin seemed determined to flout every academic convention, writing in the most esoteric of styles and prefacing his book with a willfully obscure

---

8. A less-than-satisfactory translation of this work, recently reissued, is *The Origin of German Tragic Drama* (Verso, 1999).

"Epistemo-Critical Prologue" that summarized his views on Plato, German idealism, Romanticism, beauty, works of art, language, and symbolism. The author himself described these indigestible pages to Scholem as a display of "unmitigated chutzpah" comprehensible only to students of Kabbala. Benjamin finally withdrew the dissertation when he was warned it would be rejected.

Had his professors made their way past the introduction, they would have discovered that the book was a genuinely important investigation, inspired by the work of the art historian Alois Riegl, into the allegorical dimensions of a forgotten literature. Benjamin portrays the baroque period as one of acute historical crisis, the moment when Europeans became conscious of the breakdown of the religiously ordered medieval world but before the birth of the modern. It was a time of peering into the abyss, of an awareness of the absolute separation between heaven and earth. "The hereafter is emptied of everything which contains the slightest breath of this world," and baroque man feels himself transported toward a "cataract," toward "catastrophic violence." According to Benjamin, the sorrowplays were allegories of this experience. They presented a world without order or heroes, suffused with the melancholy of statesmen, tyrants, and martyrs, who are wracked by guilt.

By his own admission, Benjamin's theological and political reflections in the *Trauerspiel* book were also inspired by the right-wing legal theorist (and later Nazi functionary) Carl Schmitt, whose *Political Theology*

had just been published in 1922.[9] Two features of
Schmitt's work evidently attracted Benjamin. One was
Schmitt's assertion that "all significant concepts of the
modern theory of the state are secularized theological
concepts." The other was Schmitt's characterization of
all legal norms as resting, explicitly or implicitly, on a
sovereign "decision," which either applied rules generally to people's actions or announced an "exception"
to them. This doctrine, which came to be called decisionism, is summarized in Schmitt's statement that
"sovereign is he who decides on the exception." The
sorrow-plays, in which princes, ministers, and even
assassins were portrayed at their moments of ultimate
decision and ultimate fate, represented baroque life just
as Schmitt imagined all political life to be: as a permanent "state of emergency."

None of these ideas appears to have surprised Scholem.
In his 1964 essay "Walter Benjamin," he wrote:

> Even in authors whose picture of the world ex-
> hibits mostly reactionary traits he heard the sub-
> terranean rumblings of revolution, and generally
> he was keenly aware of what he called "the strange

---

9. Benjamin cites Schmitt as an inspiration in a curriculum vitae, which is
translated in *Walter Benjamin, Selected Writings*, Vol. 2 (Harvard University
Press, 1999), pp. 77–79. He also made the following cryptic remark in a
diary entry of 1930: "Schmitt / Agreement Hate Suspicion" (*Gesammelte
Schriften*, Vol. II.3, p. 1,372). The large literature on the Benjamin–Schmitt
relation is summarized and analyzed by Horst Bredekamp in "From Walter
Benjamin to Carl Schmitt, via Thomas Hobbes," *Critical Inquiry* (Winter
1999), pp. 247–266.

interplay between reactionary theory and revolutionary practice." The secularization of Jewish apocalyptic doctrine is plain for all to see and nowhere denies its origin.[10]

Yet for Benjamin's friends on the left, this taste for reactionary writers was a puzzle, indeed an embarrassment.[11] Even in 1930, long after Benjamin had converted to Marxism and was collaborating with Brecht, he dedicated a copy of the *Trauerspiel* book to Schmitt, proclaiming that he found his own work on aesthetics confirmed time and again in Schmitt's writings.[12] It is not really puzzling that Benjamin should have taken such authors seriously; virtually everyone—including the avant-garde—was drinking from the same murky waters in the interwar period. The real puzzle is that he would later pursue his theological-political quest on the hard, unwelcoming terrain of Marxism.

Those who knew Walter Benjamin recognized that he underwent a conversion (his word) from theological speculation to Marxism in the 1920s, although neither they nor his later readers have ever agreed on what that conversion meant. We can date the experience to the summer of 1924, which Benjamin spent on Capri in the company of the philosopher Ernst Bloch. There he met

---

10. *On Jews and Judaism in Crisis*, p. 195.

11. For example, the Adornos silently deleted the footnotes to Schmitt in the *Trauerspiel* book when they prepared their 1955 edition of Benjamin's selected works. These have now been restored in the *Gesammelte Schriften*.

12. *Gesammelte Schriften*, Vol. I.3, p. 887.

a woman named Asja Lacis, a radical Latvian Communist who worked with Bertolt Brecht in political theater
and later became a victim of Stalin's purges and spent
a decade in a Kazakhstan camp. As we witness in his
correspondence, Benjamin immediately fell in love with
Lacis, and during their on-again, off-again affair over
the next few years he was transported into a left-wing
milieu that until then had held little interest for him.
Scholem immediately noted the change in his letters,
which now contained veiled references to Lacis. After
returning to Berlin, Benjamin tried to allay his friend's
concerns, writing that "I hope someday the Communist
signals will come through to you more clearly than they
did from Capri" and promising to explain "the various
points of contact I have with radical Bolshevist theory."
He then plunged into the study of Georg Lukács's *History and Class Consciousness* and had Lacis introduce
him to Brecht, whom he began visiting in the summer
and with whom he established a deferential relationship that had an unfortunate effect on his writing.

Benjamin's explanations and self-justifications of his
turn to Marxism continued until the mid-Thirties and
mark the high point of this extraordinary correspondence. In May 1925 Benjamin wrote to Scholem that if
his current publishing plans did not work out, "I will
probably hasten my involvement with Marxist politics
and join the party"—though he was also toying with
the idea of learning Hebrew instead; soon afterward he
wrote to Martin Buber that he was being torn between
"cultic and Communist activity." After his move to
Paris in 1926 to work on a translation of Proust, he once

again tried to explain his new thinking to the baffled
Scholem. His reasoning was anything but reassuring:

> I do not concede that there is a difference between
> [religious and political] forms of observance in
> terms of their quintessential being. Yet I also do
> not concede that a mediation between them is
> possible. I am speaking here about an identity
> that manifests itself only in the sudden paradox-
> ical change of one form of observance into the
> other (regardless of which direction), given the
> indispensable prerequisite that every observation
> of action proceed ruthlessly and with radical intent.
> Precisely for this reason, the task is not to decide
> once and for all, but to decide at every moment.
> But to *decide.* . . . If I were to join the Communist
> Party someday (something that, in turn, I am mak-
> ing dependent on one last twist of fate), my stance
> would be to behave always radically and never log-
> ically when it came to the most important things. . . .
> There are no meaningfully *political* goals.

The essential unity of the theological and political, the
"meaninglessness" of political goals, the dominance of
fate, the need for a radical, illogical decision "regardless
of the direction"—in a few sentences Benjamin summa-
rizes all the major themes of his early political writings,
though they are now presented as consistent with Marxism
rather than with the writings of Georges Sorel or Carl
Schmitt. Benjamin's Marxism first appears in his letters as
an irrational act of commitment, as an act of "decisionism."

Benjamin's attraction to Marxism was widely shared at the time, but remains a puzzle. Although his early writings had defended the independence of a spiritual realm beyond "debased" modern experience, he now called himself a materialist; after criticizing historical progress in the name of a vague apocalyptic messianism, he now called himself a Marxist supporting Communist political action. How was this possible?

Gershom Scholem thought he had the answer. As he would later write, in all messianic movements and thinkers there is a dangerous impulse to "press for the end," to try to achieve here on earth what has been promised to us only in heaven. Religious history shows that "every attempt to realize [this impulse] tears open the abysses which lead each of its manifestations *ad absurdam*." Such manifestations can develop in surprising directions as those caught up in them seek heaven on earth. Scholem had already studied how certain kabbalistic heresies in Judaism had preached a doctrine of "redemption through sin" and replaced the discipline of Torah with a mysterious anti-Torah that made material gratification a path to salvation. "Praised be he who permits the forbidden," taught the would-be Messiah Sabbatai Sevi, and the forbidden was usually profane in nature.[13]

---

13. Scholem, *The Messianic Idea in Judaism*, pp. 15, 25, 75–77. On this theme see the essay "Redemption through Sin" in that same volume and Scholem's other books, *Major Trends in Jewish Mysticism* (Schocken, third edition, 1961) and *Sabbatai Sevi: The Mystical Messiah, 1626–1676* (Princeton University Press, 1973).

Reading Scholem's historical writings along with his letters to Benjamin, we begin to understand the depth of his reaction to the latter's leftward turn. Not only was Marxism a materialistic heresy, but Scholem realized that Benjamin's genuine sacred insights would be lost in their profane transformation. And perhaps not just his insights. Benjamin gave every sign of being a man standing at the brink of an abyss, or, as one Christian acquaintance remarked, "of a person who has just climbed down from one cross and is about to mount another." Scholem was especially concerned that Benjamin would enter active Communist politics, and feared that this was not only an act of intellectual self-deception: in the political atmosphere of Weimar, it could be a threat to Benjamin's life.

Scholem put the matter bluntly in a letter of 1931:

> There is a disconcerting alienation and disjuncture between your *true* and *alleged* way of thinking. That is, you do not attain your insights through the strict application of a materialist method, but entirely independently of it [or] by playing with the ambiguities and interference phenomena of this method.... [You] could be a highly significant figure in the history of critical thought, the legitimate heir of the most productive and most genuine traditions of Hamann and Humboldt. On the other hand, your ostensible attempt to harness these results in a framework in which they suddenly present themselves as the apparent results of materialistic considerations

introduces an entirely alien form element from which any intelligent reader can easily distance himself. . . . I am so dismayed that I must say to myself that this self-deception is possible only because you desire it, and more: that it can last only as long as it is not put to the materialist test. The complete certainty I have about what would happen to your writing if it occurred to you to present it *within* the Communist party is quite depressing. . . . It would become unambiguously and explosively clear that your dialectic is not that of the materialist whose method you try to approach, at the very moment you were un-masked by your fellow dialecticians as a typical counterrevolutionary and bourgeois. . . . I fear that the high cost of this error will be borne by you. . . . You would not, of course, be the last but perhaps the *most incomprehensible* sacrifice to the confusion of religion and politics.

As it turned out, Scholem's worry that Benjamin would commit himself body and soul to communism proved unfounded. Benjamin's Marxism remained deskbound, and every encounter he had with real Communist politics left him disaffected. In the autumn of 1926 he made a brief trip to Moscow to visit Asja Lacis and, as we learn from the diary he kept there, his journey to the heart of the Revolution was a personal and political fiasco: Moscow was far from being a utopia, Benjamin spoke no Russian, and Lacis had other lovers. He had brought with him an article on

Goethe commissioned by the *Great Soviet Encyclopedia*, only to have the editors reject it as both heterodox and dogmatic. "The phrase 'class conflict' occurs ten times on every page," complained one official to his face.

An understandable chill enters the correspondence between Benjamin and Scholem during the decade following Benjamin's turn to Marxism. Still, the friends eventually found an occasion for rapprochement in the summer of 1934, when Benjamin sent Scholem a draft of his powerful essay on Kafka. The essay is perhaps Benjamin's most fully achieved attempt to blend what he called in a later letter "the experience of the modern city dweller" and "mystical experience." He writes that the stories of Kafka that have been understood as parables

> are not parables, and yet they do not want to be taken at their face value; they lend themselves to quotation and can be told for purposes of clarification. But do we have the doctrine which Kafka's parables interpret and which K.'s postures and the gestures of his animals clarify? It does not exist; all we can say is that here and there we have an allusion to it. Kafka might have said that these are relics transmitting the doctrine, although we could regard them just as well as precursors preparing the doctrine.

Scholem reported himself "98 percent satisfied" with his friend's interpretation, which presents Kafka as "feeling his way to redemption" in the modern world but failing because he finds religious tradition empty. This failure is summed up in Kafka's comment to Max Brod that there is an infinite amount of hope in the world, "but not for us."

The Kafka essay does much to confirm Scholem's claim, first made in the frustrated-sounding letters of the early Thirties and later in his memoirs, that Benjamin's most important ideas came from his concern with theological issues, while his idiosyncratic materialism only confused them. It also receives surprising confirmation from Bertolt Brecht, with whom Benjamin was staying in the summer of 1934. As we learn in the previously unpublished "Conversations with Brecht," translated in *Reflections*, Brecht, a consistent materialist, was disappointed in, and baffled by, Benjamin's theological backsliding in the Kafka essay. Benjamin faithfully reports Brecht's objection that Kafka is an "obscurantist," a "Jewboy," a "skinny, unlikable creature" whose mystical depths were at the farthest remove from the "crude thinking" the times demanded. Benjamin's celebration of Kafka's failed messianism simply advanced "Jewish fascism," Brecht charged, by fueling the bourgeois desire for charismatic leaders.

Benjamin was clearly not meant for Communist intellectual labor; his Marxism, if it can be called that, remained too intimately bound up with his original theological concerns ever to be fully disentangled. In a letter to Max Rychner of 1931 he admitted as much, even as he tried to defend his political position:

> I have never been able to do research and think
> in any sense other than, if you will, a theological
> one, namely, in accord with the Talmudic teach-
> ing about the forty-nine levels of meaning in
> every passage of Torah. That is, in my experi-
> ence, the most trite Communist platitude
> possesses more hierarchies of meaning than does
> contemporary bourgeois profundity, which has
> only one meaning, that of an apologetic.

Formulations like this placed Benjamin in an intellectual no man's land where neither Scholem the theologian nor Brecht the materialist could reach him.

Or was it a no man's land? Theodor Adorno didn't
think so. Adorno is best known today as an important
member of the Institute for Social Research, the so-called
Frankfurt School, which he officially joined in the Thirties and which since the Twenties had offered a home to
Marxists seeking a third way between Communist orthodoxy and bourgeois liberalism. He had known the older
Benjamin since their student days in Frankfurt and
greatly admired him. While indifferent to the theological interests Benjamin shared with Scholem, he took
Benjamin's turn to Marxism as a sign that a productive
secularization of his thought was underway and that
together they might develop a new theory accounting
for the diminished aesthetic experience of the modern
period. The two men were on friendly terms throughout the late Twenties and early Thirties, although they
became much closer after 1933, when Benjamin fled
Germany for Paris at the urging of Gretel Adorno.

Between his conversion to communism and his exile, Benjamin had attained some recognition as a critic in Germany. He earned a modest living by writing for newspapers and respected periodicals like the *Literarische Welt*, and by working on radio programs. This writing gave him independence and enabled him to travel widely in Europe. But when he emigrated in 1933, a few weeks after the Reichstag fire and just before Hitler assumed dictatorial powers, he had no reliable way of supporting himself. For a while he continued to write for the German press under pseudonyms, but this soon became difficult, and his commissions dwindled. To save money, he spent periods with friends on Ibiza and with Brecht in Denmark. He was even forced to swallow his pride and return for a time to his former wife, Dora, who was running a boarding house in San Remo. The last seven years of his correspondence make for distressing reading, as he hatches impractical plans for his financial salvation, and what promising opportunities arise are spoiled.

Benjamin could never have survived these exile years without Adorno's selfless efforts on his behalf. When the Institute left Frankfurt in 1933, first for Geneva, then for New York, Adorno arranged for Benjamin to receive a modest stipend for regular contributions to the Institute's journal, the *Zeitschrift für Sozialforschung*. This payment was increased when Benjamin agreed to write a long study of nineteenth-century Paris. The Arcades Project (*Passagen-Werk* or *Passagenarbeit*), as it came to be called, had begun modestly enough in 1927 when Benjamin hit upon the idea of adopting the literary montage style of the Surrealists to evoke life in nineteenth-century France. He was inspired by Aragon's reverie *Le Paysan de Paris*, which had been published the previous year and which opens with an imaginary, dreamlike tour through the Passage de l'Opéra. He first mentions an essay on the Parisian arcades in 1928, in a letter to Scholem, where he writes that he is confident of finishing it in two weeks. To everyone's dismay, the Arcades Project absorbed Benjamin's creative energies for the next thirteen years and at his death remained a chaotic ruin of notes, clippings, outlines, and fragmentary essays, all of which were miraculously preserved by Georges Bataille in the Bibliothèque Nationale during the war. Although a translation of the thousand-page morass of material is now available, readers must rely on Benjamin's last essays to get some sense of his aims.[14] In one of the most important fragments of the Arcades Project, "On Some Motifs in Baudelaire," Benjamin contrasts depleted modern experience (*Erlebnis)* with symbolically rich poetic experience (*Erfahrung*). He interprets *Les Fleurs du mal* as reflecting the disintegration of the material world's "aura," the symbolic associations that once permitted sacred objects to "return our gaze," as Benjamin puts it. In his essay on "The Work of Art in the Age of Mechanical Reproduction" (1936) he had already analyzed how modern productive forces robbed artworks of their aura, detaching them from the human traditions out of which they had emerged. The Arcades Project would try to show

---

14. *The Arcades Project* (Harvard University Press, 1999).

more subtly how the bourgeois nineteenth century had replaced the aura of the material world with a dream world, a "phantasmagoria" subtly reflecting and compensating for the contradictions of capitalist society. It would be a history of bourgeois delusions.

As originally conceived, the Arcades Project would have been much closer to the studies of dreams, archetypes, and collective memory undertaken by Klages and his followers, who had already employed the term "aura" in their work. But it soon took on a different shape and quite grandiose proportions under the influence of Adorno. When the two men discussed the project in 1929, Adorno immediately saw it as a model of his new critical theory, "the one piece of *prima philosophia* which has been given to us." He encouraged Benjamin to expand the project and to ground it more rigorously in Marx's notion of the commodity fetish. Benjamin later called this meeting the end of his "rhapsodic naiveté" and resolutely began studying Marx, whose work he knew only at second hand through Lukács. By the beginning of 1930 he could write to Scholem that the Arcades Project was "the theater of all my conflicts and all my ideas."

It became a theater of disillusionment. In 1935, in return for the Institute's support, Benjamin dutifully submitted a clear and well-organized prospectus of his work in progress, which has been translated in *Reflections* as "Paris, Capital of the Nineteenth Century." In it he carefully outlined a new kind of social history capable of embracing architecture, manners, dress, interior design, literature, photography, city planning, and much more. Citing Michelet's maxim that "each age dreams the next," he imagined that this new history would teach us "to recognize the monuments of the bourgeoisie as ruins even before they have crumbled." This short essay has proven enormously influential among contemporary historians, who by now have produced a vast, if dubious, literature on the collective unconscious of the nineteenth century along Benjamin's lines.

To read through the copious material of the Arcades Project, though, is a morbid experience. It seems less a study of the ruins of bourgeois life than the ruins of an intellectual's last productive years. The thirty-six files of quotations and aphorisms—on fashion, boredom, steel construction, prostitution, the stock exchange, the history of sects, and so on—are occasionally revealing, often funny, but generally repetitive and even dull. Yet they have been treated with all the solemnity due Pascal's *Pensées* by academic Benjaminians, who have made heroic exertions to restore this unwritten, unwritable work.

Some responsibility for the wreck of the Arcades Project must be assigned to Adorno, who in a series of long letters forced Benjamin to reconceive the project again and again. The letters make clear, however, that Adorno genuinely believed he was saving his friend from himself. Adorno, who saw the Arcades Project as a potential model for secular critical theory about bourgeois culture, worried to see it oscillating in Benjamin's hands between a vitalistic mysticism and a simple-minded Marxism. Adorno rejected the 1935 prospectus on the grounds that it was "undialectical" and that Benjamin was still "under the spell of bourgeois psychology." The letter is replete with such convoluted objections as "Haussmann's class consciousness inaugurates the explosion of the phantasmagoria precisely through the perfection of the commodity character in Hegelian self-consciousness." Later that month Benjamin replied in a sad, self-deprecatory letter (to Gretel, not Theodor), agreeing with most of the criticisms and promising to do better next time.

During the next four years, in return for his monthly payment from the Institute, Benjamin wrote regularly for the *Zeitschrift*, frequently on subjects that held little interest for him. Meanwhile the Arcades Project grew more and more out of control, even as his personal situation became increasingly precarious. In 1938, as Europe prepared for war, Benjamin submitted an enormous manuscript on Baudelaire as a miniature model of the Arcades book, only to encounter the same objections that Adorno had raised in 1935. "Let me express myself in as simple and Hegelian manner as possible," Adorno begins, without a trace of irony. He complained that Benjamin had drawn too direct a connection between the tax on wine and Baudelaire's poem about wine, in what Adorno calls "an unmediated and even causal manner." Adorno then added, unhelpfully, that "the materialistic determination of cultural characteristics is possible only when mediated by the *total* [social] *process*." Benjamin was devastated, more letters were exchanged, and a much revised version of the essay was finally published in the *Zeitschrift* in 1939 as "On Some Motifs in Baudelaire."

Though Gershom Scholem later collaborated with Adorno on republishing Benjamin's works, he always regretted Benjamin's association with the Frankfurt School, as did Hannah Arendt. While both were thankful to the Institute for supporting Benjamin financially, neither believed that Marxist critical theory was a meaningful enterprise, or that the term adequately described what was truly important about Benjamin's writings. And although Benjamin appreciated Adorno's mind, one senses in his letters a frustration with the editorial constraints imposed by Adorno and Horkheimer, which was exacerbated, no doubt, by the fact that his relation with the Institute was based on financial obligation.

We shall never know whether Benjamin's thought would eventually have developed more in Adorno's direction, fulfilling the latter's hope for a new secular, dialectical aesthetics. In the autumn of 1939 Benjamin was interned in a French camp for enemy aliens as the *drôle de guerre* began. He spent the next year desperately seeking an American visa while rejecting his former wife's pleas to join her in England. In May 1940 the Germans attacked France, and in June Benjamin fled, first to Lourdes, then to Marseilles. In August he finally received a visa with Horkheimer's help but failed to find a departing ship. Near the end of September he tried to cross the Pyrenees with a group of refugees, only to be turned back by Spanish border guards at Port Bou. That night he took an overdose of morphine and died. The next day the rest of the group made safe passage across the frontier.

Several months after Benjamin's suicide Hannah Arendt managed to escape from France to Spain. When she passed through Port Bou, she stopped to look for her friend's grave but could find no trace of it. In her baggage, however, she carried a trace of the man. It was a short essay, a sort of intellectual last will and testament entitled "Theses on the Philosophy of History," which Benjamin had given her just before his attempted flight. His expressed wish was that the essay not be published, but when Adorno received the manuscript, he decided it was too important to remain in private hands. It was first printed by the Institute in a mimeographed memorial tribute to Benjamin in 1942, and has since become one of the most controversial of his writings.

The "Theses" reflect Benjamin's apocalyptic vision of European politics in the late Thirties and his disappointment with communism's betrayal in the Hitler–Stalin pact. He had remained stubbornly, irresponsibly silent about the Moscow show trials in the Thirties, and throughout the decade could not bring himself to criticize Stalin publicly, even after Asja Lacis had been condemned to the gulag. But Stalin's pact with the devil finally shattered any illusions Benjamin may have had about communism's redemptive mission. In the Twenties Benjamin had played with the ideas of divine violence, radical decisionism, and political nihilism; in the early Thirties he could still idealize the frenzy of what he called "the destructive character." But now the real apocalypse approached, bringing with it satanic violence, not the Messiah.

At a deeper level, the "Theses" represent the last dramatic encounter between Benjamin's theological metaphysics and his historical materialism. The essay

opens with an image of the philosophy of history as a
chess game, which a puppet called historical materialism can win only "if it enlists the services of theology,
which today," he says, "is wizened and has to keep out
of sight." And what can materialism learn from theology? Essentially that the idea of historical progress is
an illusion, that history is nothing but a series of catas-
trophes piling wreckage upon wreckage, reaching up
to the heavens. The members of the working class had
been corrupted by the idea of progress, which blinded
them to the regressive social consequences that accom-
panied increased domination of the natural world.
They were lulled into ignoring the "state of emergency" caused by the rising forces of fascism, and failed
to respond. Materialism must now withdraw with
"monastic discipline" from this belief in a progressive
historical continuum, replacing it with a conception of
history closer to that of traditional Judaism, which
believed that "every second of time was the strait gate
through which the Messiah might enter." As Scholem
later remarked, nothing remains of historical materialism in this hermetic text but the term itself.

Scholem's interpretation of Benjamin as a "theologian marooned in the realm of the profane" has for
years proved a stumbling block to Marxists and critical
theorists anxious to appropriate this curious thinker's
legacy for their own purposes. Recently, as interest in
Germany's lost Jewish culture has grown, there has
been less reluctance to recognize theological elements
in his work. A somewhat hazy consensus has emerged
in German criticism, to the effect that Benjamin's

secularization left him "torn" between the sacred and profane, the metaphysical and material. As a result of this fundamental conflict in his thought, he now seems an important part of the German philosophical tradition, which has been torn between these principles ever since Kant.

But even this consensus fails to appreciate fully what Scholem's insight into Benjamin has to teach us. Whatever Scholem's illusions about Benjamin's wavering intentions to learn Hebrew or to emigrate to Palestine, he correctly saw in Benjamin the modern incarnation of the type of thinker who cannot be understood apart from traditional religious distinctions. For genuine materialists, there can be no real tension between the sacred and profane, only between illusion and enlightenment. But for the theologically attuned this tension will continue to exist as long as we must find our way in a fallen world. They may cope with it by living within law and tradition, or they may try to abolish the tension altogether. Of these, some withdraw into an otherworldly mysticism or esotericism, some throw themselves fully into the world in hopes of redeeming it with a new law, a new gospel, or a new social order. Others, like Benjamin, flirt promiscuously with both possibilities, remaining a riddle to themselves and to all who encounter them.

Chapter IV

ALEXANDRE KOJÈVE

THERE IS A celebrated passage in Turgenev's novel *Smoke* where Potugin, a cosmopolitan critic of the Slavophiles, recounts his visit to the Crystal Palace Exhibition in Victorian London. He is ashamed at not finding a single Russian invention displayed there, though hardly surprised. The problem is the Russian intellectuals, who apply themselves to universal systems of political economy but won't stoop to the practical task of washing-machine engineering. "That's beyond them," Potugin fumes. "Picking up some old cast-off shoe, dropped ages ago by St. Simon or Fourier, and sticking it on our heads and treating it as a sacred relic—that's what we're capable of."

One wonders what Sozont Ivanitch Potugin would have made of Alexander Vladimirovitch Kojevnikov, the high-born Russian who became one of the most influential political philosophers and statesmen in twentieth-century France. "Kojève," as he preferred to be called, resembled his compatriots in one important respect: he devoted the whole of his intellectual life to the recovery and explication of a cast-off philosophy, that of G. W. F. Hegel. But, unlike them, he also threw himself into the thick of practical worldly affairs, becoming an architect of postwar European reconstruction and, despite his foreign birth, a valued advisor to French presidents and ministers. It is difficult to think of a significant European thinker of the last century who played an equivalent role in the shaping of European politics, or a statesman with comparable philosophical ambitions.

For years the French claim for Kojève's importance seemed to rest on one set of lectures given to a handful of listeners during the Thirties and published by the writer Raymond Queneau in 1947. But since Kojève's death in 1968 his admirers have continued to bring out the manuscripts he left unpublished, which now constitute a rather sizable philosophical oeuvre, and he is also the subject of a major biography.[1] While his Hegel lectures were translated (in abridged form) into English more than thirty years ago, interest in his thought has not been intense in the Anglo-American world, which relegated Kojève to the class of inexplicable French enthusiasms.

In the last decade that has been changing. Francis Fukuyama's widely discussed *The End of History and the Last Man* (1992) brought Kojève's ideas about modern history and politics to a wide, if not always discerning, audience, and growing concerns about "globalization" have in the interim only rendered them more

---

1. Dominique Auffret, *Alexandre Kojève: La philosophie, l'état, la fin de l'histoire* (Paris: Grasset, 1990).

timely. Philosophically more significant was the translation of Kojève's correspondence with the political philosopher Leo Strauss, which has been published with a new edition of these two thinkers' now classic confrontation on the subject of tyranny.[2] Taken together, these materials now permit us to judge Kojève's thought comprehensively and at first hand.

Kojève was born into a well-to-do and well-connected Moscow family in 1902 and spent his first fifteen years in the cocoon of Arbat luxury. His milieu was one of great social and cultural privilege. Wassily Kandinsky was his uncle, and the entire family circulated at the fringes of the haute intelligentsia. We know little else about these early years, since Kojève was reluctant to speak of them and his biographer has conducted no original research into the period. The October Revolution extinguished the Kojevnikovs' world and subjected them to the deprivations common for families of their class: the loss of property, the vigilante murders, the blacklisting for jobs and education. Young Alexander was himself later arrested by the ruthless cheka for selling black market soap and narrowly escaped execution. He was eventually released with the help of influential family friends, but the experience marked him in a surprising way. As he later told friends, he left prison a convinced Communist, if one out of step with Bolshevik practice. In an interview

---

2. Leo Strauss and Alexandre Kojève, *On Tyranny*, revised and expanded edition edited by Victor Gourevitch and Michael S. Roth (University of California Press, 2000).

given just before his death, Kojève explained his eventual flight from Russia by admitting that, although he was a Communist, he foresaw that the establishment of communism would mean "thirty terrible years." Finally barred from all further studies, he decided to cross the Polish border with a friend in January 1920. He was seventeen years old.

After a short spell in Polish prison as a suspected spy Kojève eventually reached Germany, where he sold smuggled family jewelry to support himself while pursuing advanced studies in religion and philosophy. But in 1926 he finally settled in Paris at the invitation of his friend Alexandre Koyré, the distinguished historian of philosophy and science who had emigrated from Russia as a young man before the revolution and now taught at the École Pratique des Hautes Études. They had met a few years earlier in Heidelberg, under the oddest of circumstances. It seems that Kojève, a shameless seducer, had caused a scandal by carrying off Koyré's sister-in-law (whom he quickly married, then divorced) and the family had deputized Koyré to bring the young lady back. But on returning from his first encounter with Kojève, Koyré was so impressed that he sheepishly told his wife, "The girl is right: he's much better than my brother." Once they were together in Paris Koyré introduced Kojève into French intellectual and academic circles, inviting him to lectures and later helping him secure reviewing assignments when he was in need of cash. (Kojève's small fortune, invested in shares of the cheesemaker who used the slogan "*La Vache qui rit*," was wiped out in the crash of 1929.)

From then on Kojève's life had two, oddly juxtaposed sides: that of a reclusive philosopher and that of a high-ranking bureaucratic official. His first "life," and the better known up until now, began with his famous seminar on Hegel that dramatically shaped the French intellectual landscape of the twentieth century. The seminar began in 1933 when Koyré, who had accepted a temporary post in Egypt, asked Kojève to take over his course on Hegel's philosophy of religion at the École Pratique. Kojève, who later confessed to having read Hegel several times before then without understanding a word, decided to launch another assault on *The Phenomenology of Spirit*. This time something happened.

Hegel's *Phenomenology* attempts to give a complete and philosophically convincing account of how the human mind (or spirit, *Geist*) can, by means of reflection on its own workings, move from a simple state of consciousness of things in the world to what he called a state of "absolute knowing" in which the mind finally comes to rest, having exhausted through dialectical movement all partial and inadequate understandings of itself. One step in this developmental ladder is the moment of "self-consciousness," when the mind first becomes aware of itself as an active force, which realization leads to a bifurcation between simple consciousness and reflective self-consciousness. Hegel describes this moment allegorically as a struggle between two figures: a master (*Herr*), representing simple consciousness, who rules over and demands recognition from a servant (*Knecht*), representing the new self-consciousness. The relation between master and servant is necessarily one of conflict because, Hegel explains, it is in the nature of the self-conscious mind to want recognition from other such minds; this is its overriding desire. But at first neither master nor servant understands this desire and all its implications: the master demands recognition but denies it to the servant, whose recognition he then cannot value; the servant resents this inequality and struggles, but knows not for what, since he fails to recognize himself. In the end, the servant wins this struggle, which means, non-allegorically, that the self-conscious mind has learned to recognize itself and other such minds for what they are.

The master–servant dialectic is taken by most Hegel scholars to have an important but small place in the architecture of the *Phenomenology*. Kojève, however, was convinced not only that it was the decisive moment in that work—and, by extension, in the whole of Hegel's writings—but that it could be extended from the analysis of consciousness to that of history, whose logic it finally reveals. His argument has both Marxian and Heideggerian overtones but is wholly his own. In the lectures of the Thirties, which were published as *Introduction to the Reading of Hegel*, he carefully explained, over the course of several years, Hegel's discovery that the human struggle for recognition is the motor of all history.[3] This struggle takes place among individuals,

---

3. *Introduction à la lecture de Hegel*, edited by Raymond Queneau (Paris: Gallimard, 1947). There is an abridged English translation of this work, edited by Allan Bloom: *Introduction to the Reading of Hegel* (Basic Books, 1969).

classes, and nations; it is also staged religiously and intellectually, as men slavishly project transcendent notions of the Divine or the Good to rule over them, only to overturn those idols eventually out of the urge to self-assertion. But all these skirmishes are just part of the global human struggle, which has one ultimate aim: the satisfaction of our desire for equal recognition.

Kojève was perfectly aware that many of these notions had already been developed by the left- and right-Hegelians of the nineteenth century, and did not wish to claim any originality. He repeatedly stated that Hegel's thought was simply true but that its implications could only be understood in light of subsequent history, which is what Hegelians try to do. His only advantage was to have lived later than them and to have been privileged to see how and why history would confirm Hegel's insight, and what that implied for the future. And the most momentous implication was, quite simply, that history was finished—that ever since the French Revolution and the Napoleonic conquests modern history has been nothing but the stage on which the ramifications of these last genuinely world-historical events appeared. With the Revolution the idea of mutual recognition was established and the master–servant distinction abolished in the human mind. With the post-Napoleonic development of the modern state and economy, human beings had reached the final frontier, where they were about to become equal, satisfied citizens and consumers in what Kojève called the "universal and homogeneous state," what we today call the "international community" and the "global economy."

All the political events of the past two centuries—the wars, the conquests, the revolutions, the coups, the treaties, the massacres—were working toward this one end. "The Chinese revolution," Kojève dryly told an interviewer, "is nothing but the introduction of the Napoleonic Code into China."

For six years a small, but extremely significant, group of initiates sat at Kojève's feet while he took them line-by-line through the still untranslated *Phenomenology* and explained the end of history to them. His audience included Raymond Aron, Eric Weil, Maurice Merleau-Ponty, André Breton, Georges Bataille, Raymond Queneau, and Jacques Lacan. (Sartre, who could have learned something from Kojève, never attended.) Most of those who studied with this thirty-year-old Russian Hegelian made extravagant claims for his importance and remained loyal to him, whatever shape their own intellectual lives later took. Roger Caillois recalled his "absolutely extraordinary intellectual grip on a whole generation." For Bataille, each encounter with Kojève left him "broken, crushed, killed ten times over: suffocated and nailed down." In his memoirs Raymond Aron ranked his friend Kojève among the three truly superior minds he ever encountered.

Kojève's first "life" was transformed abruptly in 1939 when he finished his reading of the *Phenomenology* and the Germans almost simultaneously invaded Czechoslovakia. The irony was lost on no one, least of all Kojève, who would often joke about the coincidence years later. He passed the war in Marseilles where he had been prevented from continuing to the United States, and after the liberation he returned to Paris. There his second "life" began, seemingly by chance. Finding himself without employment or prospects, Kojève was asked by two of his less philosophical students to join the government as a counselor in the foreign economic relations bureau of the finance ministry. These students, Robert Marjolin and Olivier Wormser, would soon be among the most important figures in postwar French administration and diplomacy. Kojève took the job and remained a trusted government advisor until his death in 1968, and the importance of his official work is confirmed by the testimonies of Marjolin, Wormser, former Prime Minister Raymond Barre, and former President Valéry Giscard d'Estaing. Kojève all but disappeared from the Paris intellectual scene. There was a brief flurry of activity just after the war, when he published articles explaining his views in the early issues of Georges Bataille's *Critique*. And in 1947 he permitted Raymond Queneau to bring out his lecture notes from the Hegel seminar, which became the *Introduction à la lecture de Hegel*. But apart from the occasional, wickedly funny, book review, Kojève was virtually silent. When asked for revolutionary advice by leaders of the Berlin student rebellion in 1967, he replied, "Learn Greek."

The achievement of Dominique Auffret's biography is to have thrown some light on this second "life" and to have established its relation to the first. It especially helps us to place in context Kojève's mischievous remarks, attested by many friends and students, that he was "a strictly observing Communist" and "the conscience of Stalin." It must be recalled that when Kojève was developing his Hegel interpretation in the Thirties it was assumed by most European intellectuals that bourgeois democracy and capitalism were finished and would be vanquished by either communism or fascism. This was not Kojève's view. He was convinced that the entire developed world was moving, by fits and starts, toward a rationally organized bureaucratic society without class distinctions. For him it was a mere detail whether that end was to be reached through the industrial capitalism promoted by the United States (which he called the right-Hegelian alternative) or the state socialism of the Soviet Union (the left-Hegelian one). In either case, the master–servant distinction would eventually disappear and a prosperous universal state arise, satisfying our age-old yearning for recognition.

It is clear that, in the Thirties, Kojève thought the Russians had the upper hand in this struggle and he did not hide his satisfaction. But fundamentally his was a refined philosophical neutrality in what would later be called the cold war. After the Second World War he applied his talents to the protection of European, and especially French, autonomy against domination by either East or West in the historical interregnum before the universal state was established. We can now see his strategy more clearly in a recently discovered manuscript entitled "Sketch of a Doctrine of French Policy," which was written in 1945 and never published in Kojève's lifetime.[4] In it, Kojève attempts to describe

---

4. "Esquisse d'une doctrine de la politique française," *La Règle du jeu* (May 1990).

France's postwar environment and to sketch out a possible international strategy based on his reading of world history. The war itself is treated as a non-event, just a continuation of the battle between right- and left-Hegelians that began at Jena and will inevitably issue in the universal homogeneous state. The peculiar place of Europe, he asserts, was to find itself wedged between two distasteful prototypes of that state, the Soviet Union and the United States. Kojève's strategy was to create a third force by unifying Europe into what he called the new "Latin Empire," within which France would be *primus inter pares*. To that end he called for new forms of economic and political union among the Latin nations (excluding England and Germany) and close ties with Europe's colonies that were about to gain independence.

Although many of these notions were certainly in the air in 1945, this remains an extraordinarly pre-scient document. Auffret implies that some version of it must have earned him his bureaucratic post and later influenced his superiors. By collecting the testimony of many high-ranking officials and collating them with Kojève's later official memoranda, Auffret makes a plausible case for considering Kojève's ideas as im-portant sources of French policy toward Europe and the third world over the next two decades. (In the formation of the EEC and the signing of the GATT accords his direct role appears particularly convinc-ing.) The strongest single impression this tangled biog-raphy leaves is that Kojève's second "life" was a natural extension of the first, and that once he understood how Napoleon had begun the "end of history" Kojève simply resolved to help bring it about through European union and third world development.[5]

This is plausible, so far as it goes. Unfortunately, Auffret's focus on the political aspect of the Hegel-Kojève "end of history" obscures the other half of that doctrine, which is the "end of philosophy." And it is Kojève's view of philosophy, which he continued to develop privately after the war, that really deserves our attention. It was long known that Kojève would devote his weekends to writing, and was said to be composing an "update" ("*mise à jour*") to Hegel's *Encyclopedia* based on the discovery that the history of philosophy had now given way to Hegelian "wisdom." Only one obscure volume, pulled out of the middle of the manuscript, was published shortly before Kojève's death (the first part of the *Essai d'une histoire raisonnée de la philosophie païenne*), and the project seemed a failure.[6] But the appearance of the introduction to the *Mise à jour du "Système du Savoir" Hégélien* (entitled *Le Concept, le Temps et le Discours*) now completes the posthumous publication of this unfinished work.[7] When

---

5. Reports have recently surfaced that in fact Kojève may have been a Russian spy all along. A secret French government report, written in 1982–1983 and recently released, names Kojève as one of a number of top French officials with KGB connections, though the report does not offer any evidence for this charge. See "La DST avait identifié plusieurs agents du KGB parmi lesquels le philosophe Alexandre Kojève," *Le Monde*, September 16, 1999.

6. The entire *Essai* was published in three volumes by Gallimard between the years 1968 and 1973.

7. *Le Concept, le Temps et le Discours: Introduction au Système du Savoir* (Paris: Gallimard, 1990).

read along with Kojève's correspondence with Leo Strauss, it sheds great light on his announcement of the "end of philosophy" and its political implications.

Kojève said that he discovered his *"penchants philosophiques"* in 1917 when, at the age of fifteen, he began keeping a philosophical notebook that he preserved until his death. Although Auffret did not have direct access to these Russian materials, the selections translated for him by Kojève's former companion and literary executor, Nina Ivanoff, are fascinating. What they reveal is a young Russian soul thirsting for wisdom and attracted to mysticism. At a very early age he considered the possible union of Western philosophy and Eastern religion (Buddhism in particular), and in his German years began to develop a syncretic "philosophy of the in-existant" to that end. One of the strangest notebook passages reflecting this pursuit of syncretic wisdom is the transcript of an imagined "dialogue" between portraits of Descartes and Buddha, set in a Warsaw library in 1920.

Kojève subsequently spent several years studying philosophy, Oriental languages, and religion in Heidelberg, where he eventually completed a thesis under Karl Jaspers on the Russian thinker Vladimir Solovyov. Solovyov, one of the most influential thinkers in late-nineteenth-century Russia, has been described in many different ways: as a poet, philosopher, mystic, pantheist, theanthropist, theosophist. His writings try to give Schelling's "Absolute" a Christian interpretation, incorporating German idealism into Russian theology through the concept of "Godmanhood." But his notoriety also

rested on his claim to have had three mystical encounters with the feminine incarnation of *sophia* (wisdom),
once in a Russian church and later in the British
Museum and in the Egyptian desert. (These encounters
may have served as models for Kojève's Descartes–
Buddha dialogue.)

Kojève's reading of Solovyov does much to illuminate his own turn to Hegel, and it is a pity that Auffret
did not examine Solovyov's writings directly. In the
Lectures on Godmanhood (1877–1880), for example,
we already find the Kojèvian themes of the union of
East and West, of man combining divinity and nothingness, of humanity approaching absolute wisdom in
history, and of the need for a universal state. The path
from Hegel and Schelling to Solovyov and Kojève, and
back again, might appear simply circular. But what
Kojève clearly brought to Hegel was this experience
with Eastern and Christian mysticism and his study of
Solovyov. As Kojève put it in his thesis, both Christianity and Solovyov were right about everything but
the existence of an external God. The fundamental
anthropological truth of Christianity was the discovery
of man's original fall from *sophia* and the possibility of
recovering it in history, which is represented by the
Incarnation. Christianity's theism drove it to place the
Incarnation in the middle of history and then to preach
the implausible Resurrection. Hegel corrected this error
by placing the Incarnation at the beginning of the end
of history.

Kojève eventually judged his religious studies to have
been a mistake and turned instead to philosophy when

he realized that "something happened in Greece twenty-four hundred years ago, and that was the source and key to everything." If this turn from theology to the early Greeks sounds familiar, it ought to, for Kojève found himself following very much in the steps of Heidegger. Kojève's debt to Heidegger could always be surmised from his Hegel lectures, but the publication of *Le Concept, le Temps et le Discours* now clarifies the matter. Here he explains how Heidegger, like Marx before him, tried but failed to break out of Hegel's system. Once that system is properly understood, he claims, it becomes obvious that the Marxian struggle of labor and the Heideggerian encounter with death as a primordial experience were already incorporated within it—that is, that the Marxian and Heideggerian positions had been absorbed and surpassed by Hegel himself on his path to absolute knowledge. Kojève's conclusion was that the pagan pursuit of wisdom that began with the Greek philosophers had already come to an end in the logical "circularity" of Hegel's *Encyclopedia*, and that all subsequent philosophy simply depended on a partial understanding of that system. Hegel was the sage Kojève had been seeking.

Throughout the twentieth century, the "end of philosophy" was declared by any number of thinkers, usually out of linguistic or epistemological skepticism about the very possibility of a rational understanding of experience. Kojève was unique among thinkers of that century for announcing philosophy's extinction in the name of philosophy: if philosophy is the love of wisdom, we must countenance its consummation. That moment arrived with Hegel. Whether the French really understood Kojève's doctrine is unclear. After the war they abandoned Hegel in the name of Marxism and, later, structuralism, and Kojève himself withdrew into the bowels of the French bureaucracy. It now appears that the only thinker privy to Kojève's continuing private reflections on the "end of philosophy' and willing to engage him was Leo Strauss, the German-Jewish thinker whose political thought has had such deep influence in conservative intellectual circles in the United States. Thanks to the efforts of Victor Gourevitch (Strauss's former student) and the historian Michael S. Roth, the Kojève–Strauss correspondence on this issue has finally been made public, and is now printed as an appendix to Strauss's classic study *On Tyranny*.

Strauss and Kojève had met in Berlin in the 1920s when they both were pursuing studies of religion. They subsequently rejoined in Paris in the early Thirties, and later began corresponding regularly when Strauss fled to England, then to the United States. The early letters offer particularly touching accounts of the two young men struggling to adjust themselves to foreign intellectual climates. Kojève adored Paris and *la vie mondaine*, and while ironical about French intellectuals he clearly enjoyed the buzz of their conversation. Strauss preferred the breakfasts and manners of England, ranked Jane Austen higher than Dostoevsky, and ridiculed professors and intellectuals who failed to meet his philosophical standards. In one letter he scolds Kojève about a meeting in Paris, writing that "I was rather disgusted by the company in which I met you." He repeatedly objects to Kojève's friendship with Eric Weil, whose book on Hegel he called a "Prolegomena to Any Future Chutzpa." Kojève comes across as a more generous spirit and his irony is usually directed against himself. Recounting a lecture given in 1962 to a packed auditorium, he owned to feeling like "a famous twist teacher" and resolved in future to follow Strauss's advice and speak only to "the few"—but only after publishing his 2,000-page essay on Hegel's *Encyclopedia*.

Their philosophical respect for each other was unbounded. On reading Kojève's *Introduction to the Reading of Hegel*, Strauss immediately ranked it as the most brilliant case for modern thought since Heidegger's *Being and Time*, though without, he adds, "Heidegger's cowardly vagueness." Kojève returns the favor in *Le Concept, le Temps et le Discours*, writing that without meeting Strauss, "I never would have known what Platonism is. And without knowing that, one doesn't know what philosophy is."

This mutual philosophical respect arose, paradoxically, from their shared conviction that Western philosophy had reached a terminus and had to be thoroughly reconceived. Kojève, like Hegel, thought of the history of philosophy as having been driven by its dynamic relation with the history of social and political reality, each shaping the other in a steady dialectical movement toward a final resting point. When Hegel, as the story goes, saw Napoleon on horseback in Jena and understood his world-historical significance, that was the moment when philosophy reached its end. Now, according to Kojève, the task of thinking is to turn from the realm of disembodied ideas and apply itself to the more mundane task of helping to build the universal homogenous state. The history of philosophy is over; the age of Hegelian wisdom applied politically to the running of things is upon us. This is how Kojève described his own vocation in a 1946 article:

> Every interpretation of Hegel, if it is more than idle chatter, is nothing but the program of struggle and work (one of these programs is Marxism). Which means that the work of a Hegel interpreter represents a work of political propaganda.... For it could be that the future of the world, and therefore the meaning of the present and the significance of the past, depend in the last analysis on how one interprets Hegel's writings today.

Strauss drew altogether different conclusions from what he also took to be philosophy's exhaustion in the twentieth century. For him, the lesson of Heidegger's having put his philosophy at the service of Hitler was that modern thought as a whole had lost its bearings in relation to politics, and that this relation needed to be rethought in light of the classical political philosophy that the moderns had abandoned. As early as 1935 Strauss was already writing to Kojève about seeking "a radical liberation from the modern prejudice"—that is, the prejudice that the modern age has in every way progressed beyond, and is superior to, the classical world. The rest of Strauss's thinking life was devoted to analyzing the source and workings of that prejudice, and to restoring the study of classical thought so that the "quarrel between ancients and moderns" could be restaged with greater clarity about its political implications.

Kojève and Strauss agreed that choosing between ancient philosophy and modern "wisdom" would have the most profound effect on how we think and live politically. They began arguing this question in the Thirties, but it was only after the war that their debate came into focus, after the publication of Kojève's *Introduction* and Strauss's *On Tyranny*, which is a translation of, and careful commentary on, Xenophon's dialogue *Hiero*. Strauss's small volume, first published in 1948, looks at first glance to be little more than an erudite study of a forgotten work. But Kojève, who wrote a long review of it in French, immediately understood its relation to their old debate and the political experience of twentieth-century Europe. For Strauss, the most striking fact about those experiences was not that new tyrannies had arisen—tyranny is a problem coeval with political life—but that so many philosophers and intellectuals failed to recognize them for what they were. What the *Hiero* teaches, on Strauss's reading, is that philosophy must always be aware of the dangers of tyranny, as a threat to both political decency and the philosophical life. It must understand enough about politics to defend its own autonomy, without falling into the error of thinking that philosophy can shape the political world according to its own lights. The tension between philosophy and politics, even politics in its worst tyrannical forms, can be managed but can never be abolished, and therefore must remain a primary concern of all philosophers. Any attempt to flee it by withdrawing into a garden, or by putting one's mind at the service of political authority, will mean the end of philosophical reflection.

In his review article Kojève objects that Strauss is himself the victim of a prejudice, an ancient one against tyranny that fails to see how modern tyranny (he has the Soviet Union in mind) might advance the work of history and prepare the way for a better future. But, more deeply, he charges Strauss with holding to an ancient, and illusionary, conception of philosophy as disinterested reflection by individuals seeking the eternally true, beautiful, and good. Once modern philosophers realized that there were no such eternal ideas, that all ideas arise only out of the human history of struggle, they then realized that they must participate actively in history, bringing into existence the future truths that are latent in the present. Philosophers and tyrants therefore need each other to complete the work of history: tyrants need to be told what potential lies dormant in the present; philosophers need those bold enough to bring that potential out. Their relationship, according to Kojève, is a "reasonable one" understood by grownups on both sides. Of their work, only history can judge.

Strauss's reply to this challenge shows how deeply he understood the stakes in Kojève's position. How, Strauss wonders, can Kojève think that Stalin's tyranny differs morally from ancient ones, simply by virtue of its modern ideology? More deeply, how can Kojève be so sure of the wisdom of his wisdom? "Philosophy,"

Strauss asserts, "as such is nothing but genuine awareness of the problems, i.e., of the fundamental and comprehensive problems." There is something in Kojève's
manner of thinking that is deeply unphilosophical,
even inhuman—an urge to arrest the endless quest for
enlightenment, coupled with a messianic hope for the
day when human striving will cease and we will all
be satisfied. "The state through which man is said to
become rationally satisfied is," according to Strauss,
"the state in which the basis of humanity withers away,
or in which man loses his humanity. It is the state of
Nietzsche's 'last man.'"

Kojève was more than willing to accept this characterization of his position. Nietzsche was clearly on his
mind during the Hegel lectures, which is probably why
he slyly translated Hegel's German word for servant
(*Knecht*) into French as *esclave*, slave. The victory of
the servants over the masters in history will, for Kojève,
mean the victory of what Nietzsche called "slave morality," which levels all human excellence and frustrates
human striving in the name of equality and peace. In
1950 he wrote to Strauss, "In the final state there can
be no more 'human beings' in our sense of an historical
human being. The 'healthy' automata are 'satisfied'
(sports, art, eroticism, etc.), and the 'sick' ones get locked
up.... The tyrant becomes an administrator, a cog in
the 'machine' fashioned by automata for automata."

Kojève had a famous sense of humor and here, as
in many of his letters and interviews, it is not entirely
clear how serious he is being. But beneath the irony and
archness Strauss saw something that, while it earned

his intellectual respect, also horrified him. For Kojève, the prospect of men becoming less human by abandoning the quests for enlightenment or moral perfection was neither a utopian wish nor a dystopian fear; it was a possibility that history had rendered more probable, and which therefore must be reckoned with. His neutrality in the cold war between liberal-democratic capitalism and tyrannical state socialism was rooted in a deeper indifference about the potential dehumanization of his fellows, whose sufferings only concerned him to the degree that they gave rise to struggles for recognition that succeeded in shaping history. The fate of losers held no interest for him. Fortunately, Kojève was never in an official position that might have tested his nerve in this regard. But his example causes us to understand better the historical experiences of those men, Russian or not, who have treated an idea like a sacred relic and let it inspire their attempts to reshape society in its likeness.

Chapter V

MICHEL FOUCAULT

THE WORK OF Michel Foucault leaves no one indifferent. Today, nearly two decades after his death, it is still almost impossible to discuss his books and ideas dispassionately. Why should this be? Why should the writings and utterances of a sometimes obscure, always cagey thinker still stir up such strong feelings, long after he became something of a monument in the landscape of twentieth-century intellectual life?

One reason, and perhaps the most important, is that for many of his admiring readers Foucault has always been more than the author of his books. For the generation that came of age in the 1960s and 1970s he also served as an exemplar of what it is to lead an intellectually and politically serious life. This status could not have displeased him. Throughout his life Foucault claimed to be a disciple of Nietzsche, which can mean many things, but which for him seemed above all to mean that intellectual activity ought to arise out of who one is or is seeking to become, and that this is not a failing. As Nietzsche wrote in *Beyond Good and Evil*:

> Gradually it has become clear to me what every
> great philosophy so far has been: namely, the per-
> sonal confession of its author and a kind of in-
> voluntary and unconscious memoir; also that the
> moral (or immoral) intentions in every philoso-
> phy constituted the real germ of life from which
> the whole plant has grown.

In reading a Nietzschean writer like Foucault, then, we are obliged to apply Nietzsche's own dictum and judge the work not as something independent of the author's makeup and moral commitments but along with them. "In the philosopher," Nietzsche continues, "there is nothing whatever that is impersonal; above all, his morality bears decided and decisive witness to *who* he is." Therefore the first question we must ask when reading any philosopher, but especially one who has digested Nietzsche's insight, is: At what morality does all this (does he) aim?

It is to James Miller's credit that his provocative biographical study of Foucault asks this authentically Nietzschean question of its subject.[1] By treating Foucault's life, work, and death as a whole, and as part of the same quest to realize Nietzsche's ideal of an explicit

---

1. *The Passion of Michel Foucault* (Simon and Schuster, 1993). For basic biographical details Miller relies heavily on an earlier work, *Michel Foucault*, by French journalist Didier Eribon, translated by Betsey Wing (Harvard University Press, 1991). For a slightly different but very suggestive analysis of the relation between Foucault's life and work see Jerrold Seigel, "Avoiding the Subject: A Foucauldian Alternative," *Journal of the History of Ideas* (1990), pp. 273–299.

synthesis of life and work, Miller offers as strong a portrait of the thinker as we are likely to have. The story
he tells is at turns bracing, poignant, and horrifying.
We are introduced to a noble and independent spirit
who tenaciously pursued happiness as he understood
it, then see the process by which an intellectual obsession with "transgression" culminated in a dangerous
dance with death. And in between we witness him make
a foolish and fruitless detour into the politics of his
time, a detour that raises important questions about
what happens when someone takes seriously Nietzsche's
doctrine of willful self-creation and uses it to guide his
political engagements. Miller has written an important
book, a postmodern *Ecce Homo* that permits us to judge
the man and the political vision his Nietzschean morality inspired.

Foucault was born Paul-Michel in Poitiers in 1926.
His family belonged to the comfortable Catholic bourgeoisie and expected him to follow the career of his
father, a doctor whose name he bore. The war ruined
their plans. After witnessing at first hand the shame of
occupation and the hypocrisy of Vichy, Foucault left
the provinces for Paris in 1945, never to return. (He
would later drop the name Paul, further distancing himself from his father.) Miller has little new to say about
Foucault's family, and treats his arrival in recently liberated Paris as the beginning of the story. It was there
that the young student discovered philosophy under the
tutelage of Jean Hyppolite, the respected Hegel scholar
who taught in one of the schools preparing young men
for the École Normale Supérieure. These schools have

always served as important conduits of French philosophical doctrine, and Hyppolite represented the Hegelian orientation of the 1930s. But coming of age after
the Occupation, Foucault and many of his contemporaries found it impossible to subscribe to the existential
humanism that had developed in that era and which
was represented by the figure of Jean-Paul Sartre.
Although they were vaguely attracted to Marxism and
the French Communist Party, they turned their backs
almost immediately on the generation of Sartre and
Hyppolite, and began to explore thinkers whom they
considered more radical—principally Nietzsche and
Heidegger, but also avant-garde writers and Surrealists
whose hostility to bourgeois life took more aesthetic
and psychological forms.

The story of this French intellectual generation, its
confused involvement with Marxism in the decade
after the war, and its eventual development of structuralism and so-called poststructuralism, is not entirely
new. But Miller lingers over these early years in order
to examine how these developments might be related
to Foucault's more intimate experiences of the period.
Foucault was apparently miserable at the École Normale, and, despite a reputation for brilliance, was
almost universally despised and without friends. He
declared himself a disciple of the Marquis de Sade
and amused himself with gruesome Goya prints depict-
ing the carnage of war. Miller informs us that he once
chased a fellow student through the school with a dag-
ger; another day, he was found by a teacher prone on
the classroom floor, without a shirt and with razor

slashes across his entire chest. A more serious suicide attempt followed in 1948, after which he was taken to a psychiatric hospital and (like his new teacher Louis Althusser) given a private room in the school infirmary.

Delicately, but convincingly, Miller concludes that the source of Foucault's pain was a homosexuality *mal vécue*. Of course, at the time there was virtually no other way for a young French boy to live his homosexuality other than in the shadows, experiencing the shame, thrill, irony, self-hate, and hardening such a life inevitably brought with it. Miller sees its effects as being multiple and indirect. While Foucault may have seen himself as a social outcast because of his homosexuality, it was the idea of social boundaries and their transgression, not homoeroticism as such, that dominated his mature outlook. Miller is surely right, and this insight permits us to consider two separate but related themes in Foucault's life. The first, which owes a great deal to the Marx-Nietzsche mélange his generation created, was the historical analysis of how the distinctions that exist in modern society—between law and crime, sanity and insanity, order and disorder, natural and perverse—came to develop, and a (less explicit) moral critique of those distinctions as arbitrary and dubious. The second theme owes more to Foucault's discovery of Surrealist and avant-garde figures such as Georges Bataille, Antonin Artaud, and Maurice Blanchot, whose influence on this same generation is little understood outside of France. In them, Foucault saw the possibility of exploring personally what lay even further outside the bounds of ordinary bourgeois practice, to seek what he called "limit-experiences" in eroticism, madness, drugs, sadomasochism, even suicide.

Here Miller is at his most original. He has interviewed a large number of people who were involved in or could credibly recount Foucault's Dionysian explorations in these realms; he has also reexamined Foucault's writings in their light, turning up many more allusions to these experiences than we have noticed up until now. And by shuttling back and forth between the life and work, he manages to evoke Foucault's double quest: to look at modern society with the detached eye of the Nietzschean who sees the will to power at work everywhere, and to journey through the outer reaches of human experience which that society and its morality have kept from us. Except for a brief, three-year membership in the French Communist Party and an early book on psychology with Pavlovian overtones, Foucault had little to do with the Marxism and Stalinism of the 1950s. He later credited his escape to the discovery of Nietzsche's *Untimely Meditations* one summer. From that point on, he remarked, his life took a different turn, and he set out anew "under the sun of the great Nietzschean quest."

If anything, Miller might have emphasized more the apolitical, even antipolitical, character of Foucault's early orientation. This would have set into sharper contrast his later political posturing, for which he is probably best known abroad. For those introduced to him through his writings and engagements of the late 1960s and early 1970s, Foucault's later withdrawal from militancy into obscure classical texts on morals and sexuality has always seemed peculiar, and has produced an unenlightening subliterature investigating the dialectical necessity of his notorious "turns." Miller generally follows this progressive schema. But if one returns to Foucault's work and the French political context after reading *The Passion of Michel Foucault*, a rather different picture emerges. Foucault now appears as an essentially private Nietzschean moralist who began and ended his career trying to orient himself in relation to society and his own drives. The political Foucault stands out as the exception, the product of an unfortunate historical conjuncture.

Foucault's distance from French politics was initially geographic. Disappointed by the breakup of his first serious sexual liaison and feeling even further ostracized from French society, Foucault impetuously accepted a teaching post in Sweden in 1955, drawn there under the mistaken impression that Swedes were more open-minded than the French. He found himself extremely isolated, but used his solitude to begin what remains his greatest work, *Madness and Civilization* (1961). Three stifling years in Uppsala were all Foucault could bear, and in 1958 he accepted a cultural post in Poland. There he received a more brutal reminder of his social status when the Polish secret police exposed him as a homosexual in a blackmail scheme, forcing him to flee the country. He then spent two years in Hamburg and did not return to France until 1960.

Nor was he an *engagé* after his return to the hexagon. Foucault first came to public attention in 1961 as a simple scholar when *Madness and Civilization* was published as his thesis. Like its author, the book had two related sides which immediately attracted more advanced French readers. As a work of history, it recounted a fable that would reappear in many of his later works: how, at a certain point in the seventeenth century, Europeans began to distinguish diverse experiences and "practices" into rigid categories, accepting some and repressing others. In the case of madness, this meant moving from a tragic or playful view of the phenomenon to a fear of the threat *déraison* posed to modern *raison*. Then, in the late eighteenth and nineteenth century, madness (*folie*) was naturalized as a medical concept and various therapies were conceived. Lost in these developments, according to Foucault, was the premodern respect for *déraison* as a demiurgic power revealing things *raison* chose to ignore. It took the Marquis de Sade, Nietzsche, and Artaud to restore *déraison* to its proper psychological standing.

This work profoundly impressed Foucault's academic jurors. They, unlike his later disciples, agreed that it was not a conventional work of history one could take at face value, calling it "mythical" and "allegorical." Like all Foucault's books, it relies on extremely limited archival sources yet speaks in the magisterial register of World History. Its style owes more to that of Hegel and the French history of science (Gaston Bachelard, Georges Canguilhem) than to the artful Nietzsche whom Foucault wished to imitate. Still, as a work of the imagination, as a prolegomenon to future histories of madness, it is an extraordinarily rich book.

Since French readers are less than exacting about the line between history and philosophy, they were also alert to the extrahistorical (that is, moral) message of *Madness and Civilization*. It was, they saw, an advertisement for personal explorations into experiences which the modern age allegedly repressed when it accepted a clear distinction between body and mind, and between the passions of the mind and its pure faculty of reason. What are those experiences? Madness is one: "What is this power that condemns to *folie* all those who have faced the challenge of *déraison*?" Sexual violence is another: "Through Sade and Goya, the Western world discovered the possibility of surpassing reason through violence." Those who knew Foucault in France instantly saw this work as an exercise in autobiography, a Baedeker to the psychological and sexual regions he had already visited.

Foucault's reputation as an apolitical scholar continued to grow in the early 1960s. In 1963 he published both *The Birth of the Clinic* and a lesser-known study of the Surrealist writer Raymond Roussel, whose obsessions with homosexual sadomasochism, drugs, and suicide Foucault shared. There then followed the remarkable *Les Mots et les choses* (1966, translated as *The Order of Things*), a dense study of the "human sciences" whose success stunned even its author. The book remains highly seductive today, from the enigmatic interpretation of Velázquez's painting *Las Meninas* with which it opens, to the closing prophecy that man will disappear like a trace in the sand. Rhetorically, it succeeds through a kind of intellectual *surenchère*: if biology is a new science, then so is the idea of "life"; if the human sciences were invented, then so was "man";

and so on. Like *Madness and Civilization, The Order of Things* was meant to point the way out of Enlightenment humanism—which, on Foucault's understanding, propagated a mythical and oppressive view of well-ordered minds, bodies, and societies—and toward Nietzsche, Sade, and the Surrealists, who promoted a kind of moral and psychological anarchy. But with the Parisian public then groping to understand the different variants of structuralism, the book became an instant best seller, despite Foucault's polite insistence that he was not a structuralist.

Foucault's response to the publicity was revealing. He left France once again, accepting a position in Tunisia in 1967 so that he might be near the young lover who would become his lifelong companion. One wonders what would have happened had he remained there, far from the Parisian sirens. Would he have become a Gallic Paul Bowles, writing rarefied books about his experiments with drugs and sex on the African coast? We shall never know. Foucault rushed back to Paris in May 1968 when news of the "events" reached him, beginning his political detour that would not end until a decade later.

What Foucault saw, or thought he saw, in May 1968 is not hard to imagine. Until then, his Nietzschean explorations had been limited to the Bibliothèque Nationale or closed rooms. But the events of May had convinced many that the line between bourgeois normality and extreme experiences had been collectively erased by an entire generation, and that a new kind of society was in the making, one in which the working class would be joined by the "non-proletarian masses" —women, prisoners, homosexuals, psychiatric patients —to create a new, decentered society. Foucault shared this illusion for a time and threw himself into promoting it, abandoning his academic reticence for the anti-intellectual rhetoric of the propagandist. "It is not to 'awaken consciousness' that we struggle," he declared in a 1972 interview with Gilles Deleuze, "but to sap power, to take power." He added:

> In the most recent upheaval [May 1968], the intellectual discovered that the masses no longer need him to gain knowledge: they *know* perfectly well, without illusion; they know far better than he and they are certainly capable of expressing themselves. But there exists a system of power which blocks, prohibits, and invalidates this discourse.

This is the language of the new, political Foucault, who could now be seen signing manifestos, marching in demonstrations, and tossing bricks at policemen. It is also the style of the guru Foucault, who has been preserved like a lifeless mummy on American campuses, where his mystifying and contradictory interviews of the period are still consulted to divine the relation of *pouvoir* to *savoir*, *discours* to *pratique*, and *corps* to *corps*.

It was understood in France that Foucault was not a strict Marxist like Althusser, that he considered himself a disciple of Nietzsche, but it was assumed he shared the pacific and libertarian assumptions of the radical left he embraced. Miller casts doubt on this picture of Foucault's political views in the decade following 1968, and builds a convincing case that his morbid attraction to "limit-experiences" lay behind all his political engagements during these years. Whereas many of the younger generation claimed to embrace drugs, communal living, and sexual experimentation as means of escaping the grasp of "power," Foucault celebrated them as exercises in the domination of self and others, directed against "everything in Western civilization that restricts the desire for power." What lay beyond the margins of bourgeois society was not less power but more. Thus, in a 1971 televised debate with Noam Chomsky, Foucault could blithely declare:

> The proletariat doesn't wage war against the ruling class because it considers such a war to be just. The proletariat makes war against the ruling class because, for the first time in history, it wants to take power. When the proletariat takes power, it may be quite possible that the proletariat will exert toward the classes over which it has triumphed a violent, dictatorial, and even bloody power. I can't see what objection could possibly be made to this.

To speak of power and death as he did during the bloody early Seventies in Europe was no frivolous matter. The Maoist Gauche Prolétarienne, with which Foucault was associated, tore itself apart in the early 1970s over whether it should follow the examples of the

Italian and German terrorists and begin killing people. Its leader, Benny Lévy, thought he had taken the most radical position by calling for popular tribunals to judge "enemies of the people." But Foucault, who by then was professor at the Collège de France, outdid him in a famous debate by making even judicial formalities seem a bourgeois trap devised to rob the people of vengeance. "One should start with popular justice," he said, "with acts of justice by the people, and go on to ask what place a court should have in this." As if that weren't clear enough, he added that the job of the state should be "to educate the masses themselves, who come to say, 'in fact, we cannot kill this man,' or 'in fact we must kill him.' "

Miller's readers who hold to a simple view of Foucault will no doubt be disheartened by this portrait of an irresponsible Nietzschean mixing his dark obsessions into the politics of the period. But Miller is right to insist on the point, and to portray Foucault's highly influential books of that time, especially *Discipline and Punish* (1975), as shot through with violence and sadomasochism. It is hard to know what to make of this particular book, which grew out of Foucault's work with a radical prison reform group. Its underlying argument —that modern social control is all the more insidious because it is exercised invisibly and nonviolently—was hardly new to a generation convinced they were living under a reign of "repressive tolerance." Yet Foucault develops it with none of the nuance that characterized his early writings. From the opening pages, which describe in gruesome detail the flaying and quartering

of the failed regicide Damiens, there is a vitalistic revel-
ing in blood and physical cruelty that contrasts with
his demonic portrayal of how the coolly efficient institutions of modern life did their work. The fable
Foucault spins tells how social surveillance, which used
to be exercised directly and brutally, had not really
been moderated since the eighteenth century; in fact, it
had become more pervasive and insidious through indirect, mainly psychological, means of discipline in
schools, prisons, and hospitals. This new surveillance is
worse than the old, not because it perpetuates power
(power is everywhere), nor because it is held by one
group rather than another (this is inevitable), but because it works in the hidden reaches of the soul rather
than leaving its mark on the body for all to see.

Discipline and Punish, Foucault's least accomplished
historical book, has been his most influential in America,
where its allusions to hidden "power" fit so well with
the paranoid style of American politics. Miller takes it
very seriously indeed. In France, though, the reception
was different. Although there were long, respectful
reviews as soon as the book appeared in 1975, in 1974
a far more influential work on the modern prison was
published, Solzhenitsyn's *Gulag Archipelago*. The contrast between the two could not have been greater, and
muted whatever effect Foucault thought his work
might later have in France. In the face of this powerful
account of physical and mental torture directed by a
regime many in France still considered the vanguard
of social progress, it was difficult to maintain that
Western classrooms were prisons and still remain

within the bounds of good taste. Not long afterward, the boat people began fleeing Vietnam and Cambodia, and within a few years leading French intellectuals were declaring themselves opponents of anything connected with Marxism. Foucault used to provoke nervous titters by joking about cruelty and pain, but no one was laughing anymore.

The rapid political change in the French intellectual milieu in the mid-1970s had a profound effect on Foucault, more profound than Miller lets on. The reason is that Foucault was never a political leader. He was what the French call a *suiviste*: from his flirtation with Stalinism in the 1950s to his activities with the Gauche Prolétarienne in the 1970s, he simply followed the (admittedly exclusive) Parisian crowd. When it changed direction, Foucault found himself disoriented, and not just politically. Even intellectually, he seemed genuinely confused. When *The Master Thinkers*, an attack on the totalitarian temptations of modern philosophers, was published in 1977 by the former Maoist André Glucksmann, Foucault gave it a rave review, even though the book indirectly implicated his own work. In his courses at the Collège de France he soon turned away from the study of social marginalization and took up more traditional questions of political philosophy, encouraging his students to read libertarian authors on the right like Friedrich A. Hayek and Ludwig von Mises. His contradictory forays into politics continued, though. When demonstrations took place in support of the boat people or of the Polish union Solidarity, he could be counted on to be there. But when the Iranian revolution broke out in 1978 Foucault again heard the siren call of a "limit-experience" in politics, one whose consequences would ravage that country and put its people under a ruthless and narrow-minded clerocracy. He made two visits to Iran that autumn as correspondent for an Italian newspaper, exulting in the "intoxication" of revolution and the violent expression of "collective will," and praised its leaders' "political spirituality," which he thought reflected a healthy "religion of combat and sacrifice."

One could portray this change in Foucault's work and activities as merely opportunistic, given the new French concern with liberalism and human rights, and a good many in France hold this view today. But Miller is probably right to think that Foucault was in fact returning to his private moral quest. The political had once again become the personal. The catalyst appears to have been California, which Foucault began visiting in the 1970s, and where he discovered the homosexual and sadomasochistic subculture there. It was as if Sade's transgressive fantasies had suddenly become social reality for him: "These men live for casual sex and drugs. Incredible!" Abandoning the illusion of transforming modern society as a whole, Foucault now joined a smaller society of like-minded men who shared his tastes, outside the bounds of bourgeois respectability. And in his intellectual work he also returned to the unstated theme of his earliest books: sexual morality.

Miller tries hard to make sense of the last decade of Foucault's life, and partially succeeds, by treating his sexual explorations in thought and deed as deeply related. Miller speculates awkwardly about the deeds, but on Foucault's writing he is a helpful guide. With his help we can now integrate Foucault's little-understood late project, *The History of Sexuality* (3 vols., 1976–1984), into the scheme of his earlier historical and moral investigations. The first volume of this never-completed study was published in 1976 and breathes the same air as *Discipline and Punish*, full of suspicious speculations on the social "construction" of sexual identity, the "normalization" of behavior by nineteenth-century science, and so forth. But the next two volumes, which were not published until the eve of his death in 1984, are far more intimate and, in some respects, unlike anything he had ever written. To begin with, they are about sexuality in antiquity, not in nineteenth-century Europe, and they are explicitly about individual morality, an issue Foucault had studiously avoided until then.

The change in tone and orientation can be seen most clearly in the introduction to *The Uses of Pleasure*, the second volume of the history. Foucault's earlier works gave the impression, but never made the explicit claim, that the moral subject as such does not exist, that what we think of as our subjective freedom is nothing more than an effect of language and power. But now he explains how he had been led, from an investigation of the idea of sexuality in the nineteenth century, back to the history of sexual desire, then to the ways in which sexual activity had been governed by moral codes in the West, and finally to the ways in which individuals shaped themselves by accepting, rejecting, reinterpreting, modifying, and transmitting moral codes. From the study of discipline and punishment imposed on individuals he had come to see the possibility of freedom and resistance, in what he abstrusely called the "hermeneutics of the self" and the "aesthetics of existence," and which had already begun in antiquity. Foucault never criticized or retracted his earlier views about the suffocating ubiquity of social power and discipline; but now he conceded that in the face of such forces individuals still manage to develop themselves as moral beings. Ethics, it turned out, was a real subject after all, though he conceived it as an aesthetic rather than rational activity.

This aesthetic interpretation of morality goes back to Nietzsche himself, who declared in *The Birth of Tragedy* that "only as an aesthetic phenomenon can existence and the world be eternally justified." But, as Miller's book helps us to see, Foucault became attracted to two different moral-aesthetic ideals during his last years. In his research he had begun to reflect on the moderation he perceived in the Hellenistic world, and which he labeled "care of the self" or "the economy of pleasure." But in his private life he remained fixated on sexual danger and excess. Whether Foucault ever understood that his "limit-experiences" were now taking place in the midst of an epidemic is an open question, and Miller does not try to settle it. He reminds us how slow to develop was everyone's understanding of AIDS in the early 1980s. Still, the most chilling moments in the book are those where Miller recounts Foucault's profound skepticism toward the mounting scientific evidence. "*Je n'y crois pas*," Foucault told one friend in San Francisco, and he complained about gay activists who were returning to established medical "power" for help. In the autumn of 1983, after he had already collapsed and less than a year before his own death, he could still be found in the baths and bars. He laughed at talk of "safe sex" and reportedly said, "To die for the love of boys: What could be more beautiful?"

Miller takes statements like these as expressions of Foucault's attraction to suicide, though a more plausible interpretation would be that his suspicion of the "discourses" of disease and the medical "regard" had finally rendered him insensible to any distinction between a biological factum and its social interpretation. If one believes that all "discourse" about disease is constructed by social power, and that one can invent any "counter-discourse" aesthetically, it is easy to convince oneself of a certain invincibility. But Foucault was not invincible. Miller finds it merely "ironic" that the philosopher died of AIDS under medical supervision in the very hospital he had studied in *Madness and Civilization*. The word will probably have to stand, since we lack an adequate English cognate for the Greek *hubris*.

Was this the morality at which Michel Foucault's life and thought aimed—at death? Nietzsche's question haunts this whole biography and Miller does not flinch before it, though his answer—that there was "a certain dignity" in Foucault's obsession with "limit-experiences"—is certainly questionable. Still, even if we accept the coherence of his life and thought we must constantly remind ourselves that they always had one object, and one object only: Michel Foucault. Even today Foucault is remembered for his political engagements and there are many in the academy who still read a coherent, engaged, progressive, and—to use his term of abuse—humanistic political program into his work. But his life and his writings show as clearly as one could wish just what happens when an essentially private thinker, struggling with his inner demons and intoxicated by Nietzsche's example, projects them out onto a political sphere in which he has no real interest and for which he accepts no real responsibility. One might choose to follow Foucault on his inner journey, or set out on one's own, but it is dangerous and absurd to think that such spiritual exercises could reveal anything about the shared political world we live in. Understanding that world would require an altogether different sort of self-discipline.

Chapter VI

JACQUES DERRIDA

THE HISTORY OF French philosophy in the three decades following the Second World War can be summed up in a phrase: politics dictated and philosophy wrote. After the Liberation, and thanks mainly to the example of Jean-Paul Sartre, the mantle of the Dreyfusard intellectual passed from the writer to the philosopher, who was now expected to pronounce on the events of the day. This development led to a blurring of the boundaries between pure philosophical inquiry, political philosophy, and political engagement, and these lines have only slowly been reestablished in France. As Vincent Descombes remarked in his superb short study of the period, *Modern French Philosophy* (1980), "Taking a political position is and remains the decisive test in France; it is what should reveal the ultimate meaning of a philosophy." Paradoxically, the politicizing of philosophy also meant the near extinction of political philosophy, understood as disciplined and informed reflection about a recognizable domain called politics. If everything is political, then strictly speaking nothing is. It is a striking fact about the postwar scene that

France produced only one genuine political thinker of note: Raymond Aron.

The list of important French philosophers who protected their work from the political passions of the day is short, though it contains some significant figures. One thinks of the Jewish moral philosopher Emmanuel Lévinas, the misanthropic essayist E. M. Cioran, and the father of deconstruction, Jacques Derrida. This claim about Derrida may surprise American readers, given the ideologically charged atmosphere in which his work has been received on our side of the Atlantic, but it is true—or at least was true until quite recently. Unlike so many of his fellow students at the École Normale Supérieure in the Fifties, Derrida kept clear of the Stalinized French Communist Party (PCF), and later adopted a skeptical attitude toward the events of May 1968 and the short-lived hysteria for Mao. Over the next decade, as Michel Foucault became the great white hope of the post-1968 left, Derrida frustrated all attempts to read a simple political program into deconstruction. He declared himself to be a man of the left but refused to elaborate, leaving more orthodox thinkers to wonder whether deconstruction reflected anything more than "libertarian pessimism," as the Marxist critic Terry Eagleton once charged.

As Derrida's star began to fall in France in the 1980s, it was rising in the English-speaking world, where questions about his political commitments were raised anew. This must have been awkward for him on several counts. Derrida's thought is extremely French in its themes and rhetoric, and is difficult to understand outside the context of long-standing Parisian disputes over the legacies of structuralism and Heideggerianism. In the United States, however, his ideas, which were first introduced into literary criticism, now circulate in the alien environment of academic postmodernism, which is a loosely structured constellation of ephemeral disciplines like cultural studies, feminist studies, gay and lesbian studies, science studies, and postcolonial theory. Academic postmodernism is nothing if not syncretic, which makes it difficult to understand or even describe. It borrows notions freely from the (translated) works of Derrida, Michel Foucault, Gilles Deleuze, Jean-François Lyotard, Jean Baudrillard, Julia Kristeva —and, as if that were not enough, also seeks inspiration from Walter Benjamin, Theodor Adorno, and other figures from the German Frankfurt School. Given the impossibility of imposing any logical order on ideas as dissimilar as these, postmodernism is long on attitude and short on argument. What appears to hold it together is the conviction that promoting these very different thinkers somehow contributes to a shared emancipatory political end, which remains conveniently ill-defined.

In America, Derrida is considered a classic of the postmodern canon. But as recently as 1990 he still declined to explain the political implications of deconstruction. Occasionally a book would appear claiming to have cracked the code and discovered hidden affinities between deconstruction and, say, Marxism or feminism. The Sphinx just grinned. But now, at long last, Jacques Derrida has spoken—and spoken, publishing no fewer than six books on political themes over the past decade. Some are no more than pamphlets and interviews, but three of them—a book on Marx, one on friendship and politics, another on law—are substantial treatises. Why Derrida has chosen this particular moment to make his political debut is a matter of speculation. His thoughts could not be more out of season in France, and his six books met bafflement when they appeared there. But given the continuing influence of postmodernism in the United States, where Derrida now spends much of his time teaching, his interventions could not be more timely. They give us plenty of material for reflection about the real political implications of deconstruction and whether American readers have quite grasped them.

On or about November 4, 1956, the nature of French philosophy changed. That, in any case, is what the textbooks tell us. In the decade following the Liberation, the dominant presence in French philosophy was Jean-Paul Sartre and the dominant issue was communism. Sartre's *L'Être et le néant* (1943) had earned him a reputation as an existentialist during the Occupation, and his famous lecture of 1945, "L'Existentialisme est un humanisme," brought an assertive humanism to a wide European audience at war's end. Yet within a few years of having spoken out on behalf of absolute human liberty, Sartre became an obedient fellow traveler. In his infamous tract "Les Communistes et la paix," which began to be serialized in 1952, he dismissed reports of the gulag, and after a trip to the Soviet Union in 1954 declared in an interview that "the freedom to criticize is total in the USSR." Having once extolled man's unique

capacity for free choice, Sartre announced a decade
later that Marxism was the unsurpassable horizon of
our time.

But in 1956 (so the story goes) the myth of the Soviet
Union was shattered in France by Khrushchev's secret
speech to the Twentieth Party Conference in Moscow
in February and the suppression of the Hungarian
revolt that autumn. This brought an end to many illusions: about Sartre, about communism, about history,
about philosophy, and about the term "humanism." It
also established a break between the generation of
French thinkers reared in the Thirties, who had seen
the war as adults, and students who felt alien to those
experiences and wished to escape the suffocating
atmosphere of the cold war. The latter therefore turned
from the "existential" political engagement recommended by Sartre toward a new social science called
structuralism. And (the story ends) after this turn there
would develop a new approach to philosophy, of which
Michel Foucault and Jacques Derrida are perhaps the
most distinguished representatives.

The problem with this textbook history is that it
vastly overstates the degree to which French intellectuals stripped themselves of their Communist illusions in
1956. What it gets right is the role of structuralism in
changing the terms in which political matters generally
were discussed. Structuralism was a term coined by
the anthropologist Claude Lévi-Strauss to describe a
method of applying models of linguistic structure to
the study of society as a whole, in particular to customs
and myths. Though Lévi-Strauss claimed inspiration

from Marx, he interpreted Marxism to be a science of society, not a guide to political action.

Sartre's engaged Marxist humanism rested on three basic presuppositions: that history's movements can be understood rationally; that those movements are determined by class relations; and that the individual's responsibility was to further human emancipation by assisting progressive class forces. Lévi-Strauss drew two very different principles from reading Marx in light of the French sociological tradition (especially the works of Émile Durkheim) and his own anthropological fieldwork. They were that societies are structures of relatively stable relations among their elements, which develop in no rational historical pattern, and that class has no special status among them. As for man's existential responsibilities, Lévi-Strauss had nothing to say. It was a provocative silence. For if societies were essentially stable structures whose metamorphoses were unpredictable, that left little room for man to shape his political future through action. Indeed, man seemed rather beside the point. As Lévi-Strauss put it in his masterpiece *Tristes Tropiques* (1955), "The world began without the human race, and it will end without it."

Today it is somewhat difficult to understand how this austere doctrine could have appealed to young people caught up in the cold war atmosphere of the Fifties. It helps to realize how profoundly Lévi-Strauss was attacking the defining myth of modern French politics. Beginning in the Third Republic there developed a shaky political consensus in France, to the effect that the Declaration of the Rights of Man pronounced in

1789 reflected universal truths about the human condition, which France had been anointed to promulgate to the world. After two world wars, the Occupation, and Vichy, this myth of universalism in one country struck many young Frenchmen as absurd. Lévi-Strauss's structuralism cast doubt on the universality of any political rights or values, and also raised suspicions about the "man" who claimed them. Weren't these concepts simply a cover for the West's ethnocentrism, colonialism, and genocide, as Lévi-Strauss charged? And wasn't Sartre's Marxism polluted by the same ideas? Marxism spoke of each nation's place in the general unfolding of history; structuralism spoke of each culture as autonomous. Marxism preached revolution and liberation for all peoples; structuralism spoke of cultural difference and the need to respect it. In the Paris of the late Fifties, the cool structuralism of Lévi-Strauss seemed at once more radically democratic and less naive than the engaged humanism of Sartre.

Besides, structuralist concern with "difference" and the "Other" also had a strong political effect in the decade of decolonization and the Algerian War. Lévi-Strauss's most significant works were all published during the breakup of the French colonial empire and contributed enormously to the way it was understood by intellectuals. Sartre was much engaged in anticolonial politics and saw in third world revolutions the birth of a "new man," as he put it in his passionate preface to Frantz Fanon's *Les Damnés de la terre* (1961). Lévi-Strauss never engaged in polemics over decolonization or the Algerian War. Nonetheless, his elegant writings worked an aesthetic transformation on his readers, who were subtly made to feel ashamed to be European. Using the rhetorical gifts he learned from Rousseau, he evoked the beauty, dignity, and irreducible strangeness of third world cultures that were simply trying to preserve their difference. And though Lévi-Strauss may not have intended it, his writings would soon feed the suspicion among the New Left that grew up in the Sixties that all the universal ideas to which Europe claimed allegiance—reason, science, progress, liberal democracy—were culturally specific weapons fashioned to rob the non-European Other of his difference.

As François Dosse shows in his useful new study of structuralism, the movement had a lasting impact on French thought and intellectual politics, even though its doctrines were quickly misunderstood and misapplied in the next generation.[1] For Lévi-Strauss, structuralism was a scientific method for studying differences between cultures, in the hope of one day achieving a more genuinely universal understanding of human nature. For the *tiers-mondistes* he inspired, and who were radicalized by the Algerian War, this scientific relativism degenerated into just another primitivism that neutralized any criticism of abuses within foreign cultures. (Not to mention the crimes of Communist totalitarianism, which now could be excused on culturalist rather than

---

1. François Dosse, *History of Structuralism*, 2 volumes (University of Minnesota Press, 1997). This next generation is usually called "poststructuralist" in English to mark the break with structuralism's original scientific program. This term is not used in French, however, and Dosse employs "structuralism" to refer to the entire movement. I follow him in this.

Stalinist grounds.) As the Sixties progressed, the children of structuralism came to forget Lévi-Strauss's skepticism about the French revolutionary myth and began promoting the Other as an honorary *sans culottes*. All that was marginal within Western societies could now be justified and even celebrated philosophically. Some followed Michel Foucault in portraying the development of European civilization as a process of marginalizing domestic misfits—the mentally ill, sexual and political deviants—who were branded and kept under surveillance through the cooperation of social "power" and "knowledge." Others turned to psychology, searching for the repressed Other in the libido or the unconscious.

By the mid-Seventies the structuralist idea had declined from a scientific method informed by political and cultural pessimism into a liberation anti-theology celebrating difference wherever it might be found. In one sense, then, little had changed since 1956. French intellectuals still thought of themselves on the Dreyfusard model, and philosophers continued to write thinly veiled political manifestoes. But the structuralist experience had changed the terms in which political engagements were conceived philosophically. It was no longer possible to appeal to a rational account of history, as Sartre had, to justify political action. It was not clear that one could appeal to reason at all, since language and social structure loomed so large. One could not even speak of man without putting the term in quotation marks. "Man" was now considered a site, a point where various social, cultural, economic, linguistic, and psychological forces happened to intersect. As Michel

Foucault put it in the closing sentence of *The Order of Things* (1966), man was a recent invention that would soon disappear, like a face drawn in the sand.

That surely was not what Lévi-Strauss had in mind when he spoke of creation outlasting man, but the die was already cast. What this radical antihumanism would mean for politics was not altogether clear. For if "man" was entirely a construct of language and social forces, then how was *homo politicus* to deliberate on and justify his actions? Whatever one thought of Sartre's political engagements, he had an answer to that question. The structuralists did not.

François Dosse describes Jacques Derrida's doctrine of deconstruction as an "ultrastructuralism." This is accurate enough but does not tell the whole story. In France at least, the novelty of deconstruction in the Sixties was to have addressed the themes of structuralism—difference, the Other—with the philosophical concepts and categories of Martin Heidegger. Derrida's early writing revived a *querelle* over the nature of humanism, which had set Heidegger against Sartre back in the late Forties and had many political implications. Derrida sided with Heidegger, whom he only criticized for not having gone far enough. And it is to that decision in favor of Heidegger that all the political problems of deconstruction may be traced.

The Sartre–Heidegger dispute followed Sartre's 1945 lecture on humanism, which Heidegger read as a travesty of his own intellectual position. Sartre had appropriated the Heideggerian language of anxiety, authenticity, existence, and resolution to make the case that, in

the words of Francis Ponge, "man is the future of man"
—that is, that man's autonomous self-development
should replace transcendent ends as the aim of all our
striving. In a long, and justly famous, "Letter on Humanism" (1946), Heidegger responded that his aim had
always been to question the concept of man and perhaps free us from it. Ever since Plato, he wrote, Western
philosophy had made unexamined metaphysical assumptions about man's essence that disguised the fundamental question of Being and placed man himself at the
center of creation. All the scourges of modern life—science, technology, capitalism, communism—could be
traced back to this original "anthropologization" of
Being. This was a heavy burden, which could only be
lifted through the dismantling (*Destruktion*) of the metaphysical tradition. Only then could man learn that he is
not the master but rather the "shepherd" of Being.

Deconstruction was conceived in the spirit of Heidegger's *Destruktion*, though Derrida had no intention
of making man the shepherd of anything. In a remarkable lecture in 1968, "The Ends of Man," Derrida
pointed out that by anointing man the "shepherd of
Being," Heidegger had returned to humanism "as if by
magnetic attraction." He then claimed that the metaphysical tradition could only really be overcome if
the very language of philosophy was "deconstructed,"
a language in which even Heidegger was snared. At the
root of the metaphysical tradition was a naive notion
of language as a transparent medium, a "logocentrism,"
as Derrida dubbed it. The Greek term *logos* means word
or language, but it can also mean reason or principle—

an equation of speech with intentionality that Derrida considered highly questionable. What was needed was a radical "decentering" of the implicit hierarchies imbedded in this language that encourage us to place speech above writing, the author above the reader, or the signified above the signifier. Deconstruction thus was described as a prolegomenon to—or perhaps even a substitute for—philosophy as traditionally conceived. It would be an activity allowing the aporias, or paradoxes, imbedded in every philosophical text to emerge without forcing a "violent" consistency upon them. The end of logocentrism would then mean the end of every other wicked "centrism": androcentrism, phallocentrism, phallologocentrism, carnophallologocentrism, and the rest. (All these terms appear in Derrida's books.)

As a specimen of *normalien* cleverness, Derrida's attack on his intellectual forefathers could hardly be bettered. He accused both structuralists and Heidegger of not having pushed their own fundamental insights far enough. Structuralists destabilized our picture of man by placing him in a web of social and linguistic relations, but then assumed that web of relations—structures—to have a stable center. Heidegger's blindness to his own language led from the *Destruktion* of metaphysics to the promotion of man as the "shepherd of Being." Derrida's contribution, if that is the correct term, was to have seen that by pressing further the antihumanism latent in both these intellectual traditions, he could make them seem compatible ways of addressing logocentrism.

But having done that, Derrida then found himself bound to follow the linguistic principles he had discovered in his campaign against logocentrism, especially the hard doctrine that since all texts contain ambiguities and can be read in different ways (*la différence*), exhaustive interpretation must be forever deferred (*la différance*). That raised the obvious question: How then are we to understand deconstruction's own propositions? As more than one critic has pointed out, there is an unresolvable paradox in using language to claim that language cannot make unambiguous claims. For Derrida coping with such evident paradoxes is utterly beside the point. As he has repeatedly explained, he conceives of deconstruction less as a philosophical doctrine than as a "practice" aimed at casting suspicion on the entire philosophical tradition and robbing it of self-confidence.

Anyone who has heard him lecture in French knows that he is more performance artist than logician. His flamboyant style—using free association, rhymes and near-rhymes, puns, and maddening digressions—is not just a vain pose (though it is surely that). It reflects what he calls a self-conscious "acommunicative strategy" for combating logocentrism. As he puts it in the interview published in *Moscou aller-retour*:

> What I try to do through the neutralization of communication, theses, and stability of content, through a microstructure of signification, is to provoke, not only in the reader but also in oneself, a new tremor or a new shock of the body that opens a new space of experience. That might

explain the reaction of not a few readers when they say that, in the end, one doesn't understand anything, there's no conclusion drawn, it's too sophisticated, we don't know if you are for or against Nietzsche, where you stand on the woman question. . . .[2]

It also might explain the reaction of those readers who suspect that the neutralization of communication means the neutralization of all standards of judgment —logical, scientific, aesthetic, moral, political—and leaves these fields of thought open to the winds of force and caprice. Derrida always brushed aside such worries as childish, and in the atmosphere of the Sixties and Seventies few questions were asked. But the Eighties proved to be trying times for deconstruction. In 1987 a Chilean writer named Victor Farías published a superficial book on Martin Heidegger's involvement with the Nazis and its alleged roots in his philosophy. While the book contained no major revelations, it was taken in France and Germany to confirm the suspicion that, to the extent that philosophy in the Sixties and Seventies was Heideggerian, it was politically irresponsible. Jacques Derrida rejected these associations out of hand.[3]

But that same year it was also revealed that the late Yale professor Paul de Man, a leading champion of

---

2. *Moscou aller-retour* (La Tour d'Aigues: Éditions de l'Aube, 1995), p. 146.

3. See Thomas Sheehan, "A Normal Nazi," *The New York Review of Books*, January 14, 1993, as well as letters from Derrida, Richard Wolin, and others in *The New York Review of Books*, February 11, March 4, and March 25, 1993.

deconstruction and close friend of Derrida's, had published collaborationist and anti-Semitic articles in two
Belgian newspapers in the early Forties. These might
have been dismissed as youthful errors had Derrida and
some of his American followers not then interpreted
away the offending passages, denying their evident
meaning, leaving the impression that deconstruction
means you never have to say you're sorry.[4] It now
appeared that deconstruction had, at the very least, a
public relations problem, and that the questions of
politics it so playfully left in suspension would now
have to be answered.

Yet how would that be possible? Derrida's radical
interpretations of structuralism and Heideggerianism
had rendered the traditional vocabulary of politics un-
usable and nothing could be put in its place. The subjects considered in traditional political philosophy—
individual human beings and nations—were declared
to be artifices of language, and dangerous ones at that.
The object of political philosophy—a distinct realm of
political action—was seen as part of a general system
of relations that itself had no center. And as for the
method of political philosophy—rational inquiry toward
a practical end—Derrida had succeeded in casting suspicion on its logocentrism. An intellectually consistent
deconstruction would therefore seem to entail silence
on political matters. Or, if silence proved unbearable, it
would at least require a serious reconsideration of the

---

4. For a full account, with references, see Louis Menand, "The Politics of
Deconstruction," *The New York Review of Books*, November 21, 1991.

antihumanist dogmas of the structuralist and Heideggerian traditions. To his credit, Michel Foucault began such a reconsideration in the decade before his death. Jacques Derrida never has.

The most we are ever likely to learn about Derrida's understanding of strictly political relations is contained in *Politics of Friendship*—the only one of his books with the word "politics" in the title.[5] It is based on a seminar given in Paris in 1988–1989, just as Europe was being shaken to its foundation by the rapid collapse of the Eastern bloc. As it happens, I attended this seminar and, like most of the participants I met, had difficulty understanding what Derrida was driving at. Each session would begin with the same citation from Montaigne—"*O mes amis, il n'y a nul ami*" ("O my friends, there is no friend")—and then veer off into a rambling discussion of its possible sources and meanings. The published text is much reworked and gives a clearer picture of what Derrida has in mind.

His aim is to show that the entire Western tradition of thinking about politics has been distorted by our philosophy's *peccatum originarium*, the concept of identity. Because our metaphysical tradition teaches that man is identical to himself, a coherent personality free from internal difference, we have been encouraged to seek our identities through membership in undifferentiated, homogenizing groups such as families, friendships, classes, and nations. From Aristotle to the French Revolution, the good republic has therefore

---

5. *Politics of Friendship* (Verso, 1997).

been thought to require *fraternité*, which is idealized as a natural blood tie making separate individuals somehow one. But there is no such thing as natural fraternity, Derrida asserts, just as there is no natural maternity [*sic*]. All such natural categories, as well as the derivative concepts of community, culture, nation, and borders, are dependent on language and therefore are conventions. The problem with these conventions is not simply that they cover up differences within the presumably identical entities. It is that they also establish hierarchies among them: between brothers and sisters, citizens and foreigners, and eventually friends and enemies. In the book's most reasoned chapters, Derrida examines Carl Schmitt's conception of politics, which portrays the political relation as an essentially hostile one between friends and enemies. Derrida sees Schmitt not as a mere Nazi apologist with a thirst for conflict, but as a deep thinker who made explicit the implicit assumptions of all Western political philosophy.

From this point of view it would seem that all Western political ideologies—fascism, conservatism, liberalism, socialism, communism—would be equally unacceptable. That is the logical implication of Derrida's attack on logocentrism, and sometimes he appears to accept it. In *Specters of Marx* and *The Other Heading* he denounces the new liberal consensus he sees as having ruled the West since 1989, lashing out hysterically, and unoriginally, at the "New International" of global capitalism and media conglomerates that have established world hegemony by means of an "unprecedented form of war."[6] He is less critical of Marxism (for reasons we will examine), though he does believe that communism became totalitarian when it tried to realize the eschatological program laid out by Marx himself. Marx's problem was that he did not carry out fully his own critique of ideology and remained within the logocentrist tradition. That is what explains the gulag, the genocides, and the terror carried out in his name by the Soviet Union. "If I had the time," Derrida tells his undoubtedly stupefied Russian interviewers in *Moscou aller-retour*, "I could show that Stalin was 'logocentrist,'" though he admits that "that would demand a long development."

It probably would. For it would mean showing that the real source of tyranny is not tyrants, or guns, or wicked institutions. Tyranny begins in the *language* of tyranny, which derives ultimately from philosophy. If that were transformed, or "neutralized" as he says in *Politics of Friendship*, so eventually would our politics be. He proves to be extremely open-minded about what this might entail. He asks rhetorically whether "it would still make sense to speak of democracy when there would be no more speaking of country, nation, even state and citizen." He also considers whether the abandonment of Western humanism would mean that concepts of human rights, humanitarianism, even crimes against humanity would have to be forsworn.

---

6. *Specters of Marx: The State of the Debt, the Work of Mourning, and the New International* (Routledge, 1994); *The Other Heading: Reflections on Today's Europe* (Indiana University Press, 1992).

But then what remains? If deconstruction throws doubt on every political principle of the Western philosophical tradition—Derrida mentions propriety, intentionality, will, liberty, conscience, self-consciousness, the subject, the self, the person, and community—are judgments about political matters still possible? Can one still distinguish rights from wrongs, justice from injustice? Or are these terms, too, so infected with logocentrism that they must be abandoned? Can it really be that deconstruction condemns us to silence on political matters, or can it find a linguistic escape from the trap of language?

Readers of Derrida's early works can be forgiven for assuming that he believes there can be no escape from language, and therefore no escape from deconstruction for any of our concepts. His achievement, after all, was to have established this hard truth, which was the only truth he did not question. But in the Nineties Jacques Derrida changed his mind, and in a major way. It turns out that there is a concept—though only one—resilient enough to withstand the acids of deconstruction, and that concept is "justice."

In the autumn of 1989 Derrida was invited to address a symposium in New York on the theme "deconstruction and the possibility of justice." His lecture has now been expanded in a French edition and published along with an essay on Walter Benjamin.[7] Derrida's aim in the

---

7. *Force de loi* (Paris: Éditions Galilée, 1994). The original lecture appeared in Drucilla Cornell, et al., editors, *Deconstruction and the Possibility of Justice* (Routledge, 1992).

lecture is to demonstrate that although deconstruction can and should be applied to the law, it cannot and should not be taken to undercut the notion of justice. The problem with law, in his view, is that it is founded and promulgated on the basis of authority, and therefore, he asserts (with typical exaggeration), depends on violence. Law is affected by economic and political forces, is changed by calculation and compromise, and therefore differs from place to place. Law is written into texts and must be interpreted, which complicates things further.

Of course, none of this is news. Our whole tradition of thinking about law, beginning in Greek philosophy and passing through Roman law, canon law, and modern constitutionalism, is based on the recognition that laws are a conventional device. The only controversial issue is whether there is a higher law, or right, by which the conventional laws of nations can be judged, and, if so, whether it is grounded in nature, reason, or revelation. This distinction between law and right is the foundation of Continental jurisprudence, which discriminates carefully between *loi/droit*, *Gesetz/Recht*, *legge/diritto*, and so forth. Derrida conflates *loi* and *droit* for the simple reason that he recognizes neither nature nor reason as standards for anything. In his view, both are caught up in the structures of language, and therefore may be deconstructed.

Now, however, he also wishes to claim that there is a concept called justice, and that it stands "outside and beyond the law." But since this justice cannot be understood through nature or reason, that only leaves one

possible means of access to its meaning: revelation.
Derrida studiously avoids this term but it is what he is
talking about. In *Force de loi* he speaks of an "idea of
justice" as "an experience of the impossible," something that exists beyond all experience and therefore
cannot be articulated. And what cannot be articulated
cannot be deconstructed; it can only be experienced in
a mystical way. This is how he puts it:

> If there is deconstruction of all determining pre-
> sumption of a present justice, it operates from an
> infinite "idea of justice," infinitely irreducible. It
> is irreducible because due to the Other—due to
> the Other before any contract, because this idea
> has arrived, the arrival of the Other as a singular-
> ity always Other. Invincible to all skepticism...
> this "idea of justice" appears indestructible....
> One can recognize, and even accuse it of madness.
> And perhaps another sort of mysticism. Decon-
> struction is mad about this justice, mad with the
> desire for justice.

Or again in *Specters of Marx*:

> What remains irreducible to any deconstruction,
> what remains as indeconstructible as the possibil-
> ity itself of deconstruction, is, perhaps, a certain
> experience of the emancipatory promise; it is per-
> haps even the formality of a structural messianism,
> a messianism without religion, even a messianic
> without messianism, an idea of justice—which we

distinguish from law or right and even from human rights—and an idea of democracy which we distinguish from its current concept and from its determined predicates today.

There is no justice present anywhere in the world. There is, however, as Derrida puts it, an "infinite idea of justice," though it cannot and does not penetrate our world. Yet this necessary absence of justice does not relieve us of the obligation to await its arrival, for the Messiah may come at any moment, through any city gate. We must therefore learn to wait, to defer gratifying our desire for justice. And what better training in deferral than deconstruction? If deconstruction questions the claim of any law or institution to embody absolute justice, it does so in the very name of justice—a justice it refuses to name or define, an "infinite justice that can take on a 'mystical' aspect." Which leads us, without surprise, to the conclusion that "*deconstruction is justice.*"

Socrates equated justice with philosophy, on the grounds that only philosophy could see things as they truly are, and therefore judge truly. Jacques Derrida, mustering all the chutzpah at his disposal, equates justice with deconstruction, on the grounds that only the undoing of rational discourse about justice will prepare the advent of justice as Messiah.

How seriously are we meant to take all this? As always with Derrida it is difficult to know. In recent books he borrows freely from the modern messianic writings of Emmanuel Lévinas and Walter

Benjamin. But whatever one makes of these two thinkers, they had too much respect for theological concepts like promise, covenant, Messiah, and anticipation to throw these words about cavalierly. Derrida's turn to them in these new political writings bears all the signs of intellectual desperation. He clearly wants deconstruction to serve some political program, and to give hope to the dispirited left. He also wants to correct the impression that his own thought, like that of Heidegger, leads inevitably to a blind "resolve," an assertion of will that could take any political form. As he remarked not long ago, "My hope as a man of the left, is that certain elements of deconstruction will have served or—because the struggle continues, particularly in the United States —*will* serve to politicize or repoliticize the left with regard to positions which are not simply academic."[8] Yet the logic of his own philosophical arguments, such as they are, proves stronger than Derrida. He simply cannot find a way of specifying the nature of the justice to be sought through left-wing politics without opening himself to the very deconstruction he so gleefully applies to others. Unless, of course, he places the "idea of justice" in the eternal, messianic beyond where it cannot be reached by argument, and assumes that his ideologically sympathetic readers won't ask too many questions.

But politics on the left, no less than on the right, is not a matter of passive expectation. It envisages action. And if the idea of justice cannot be articulated, it cannot

---

8. "Remarks on Deconstruction and Pragmatism," in Chantal Mouffe, editor, *Deconstruction and Pragmatism* (Routledge, 1996), pp. 77–86.

provide any aim for political action. According to Derrida's argument, all that remains to guide us is decision, pure and simple: a decision for justice or democracy, and for a particular understanding of both. Derrida places enormous trust in the ideological goodwill or prejudices of his readers, for he cannot tell them why he chooses justice over injustice, or democracy over tyranny, only that he does. Nor can he offer the uncommitted any reasons for thinking that the left has a monopoly on the correct understanding of these ideas. He can only offer impressions, as in the little memoir he has published in *Moscou aller-retour*, where he confesses to still being choked with emotion whenever he hears the *Internationale*.

This nostalgic note is struck time and again in *Specters of Marx* and *Moscou aller-retour*, which deserve permanent places in the crowded pantheon of bizarre Marxist apologetics. In the latter book Derrida declares that "deconstruction never had meaning or interest, at least in my eyes, than as a radicalization, that is to say, also *within the tradition* of a certain Marxism, in a certain *spirit of Marxism*." Not, of course, that he wishes to defend anything Marx himself actually wrote or believed. He declares Marx's economics to be rubbish and his philosophy of history a dangerous myth. But all that is beside the point. The "spirit" of Marxism gave rise to a great heritage of messianic yearning, and deserves respect for that reason. Indeed, in a certain sense, we are all Marxists now simply because Marxism, well, happened:

Whether they wish it or know it or not, all men and women, all over the earth, are today to a certain extent the heirs of Marx and Marxism. That is, as we were saying a moment ago, they are heirs of the absolute singularity of a project—or of a promise—which has a philosophical and scientific form. This form is in principle non-religious, in the sense of a positive religion; it is not mythological; it is therefore not national—for beyond even the alliance with a chosen people, there is no nationality or nationalism that is not religious or mythological, let us say "mystical" in the broad sense. The form of this promise or of this project remains absolutely unique. . . .

Whatever one may think of this event, of the sometimes terrifying failure of that which was thus begun, of the techno-economic or ecological disasters, and the totalitarian perversions to which it gave rise, . . . whatever one may think also of the trauma in human memory that may follow, this unique attempt took place. A messianic promise, even if it was not fulfilled, at least in the form in which it was uttered, even if it rushed headlong toward an ontological content, will have imprinted an inaugural and unique mark in history. And whether we like it or not, whatever consciousness we have of it, we cannot not be its heirs.

With statements like these Jacques Derrida risks giving bad faith a bad name. The simple truth is that his

thinking has nothing to do with Marx or Marxism.
Derrida is some vague sort of left democrat who values
"difference" and, as his recent short pamphlet on cos-
mopolitanism shows, he is committed to seeing Europe
become a more open, hospitable place, not least for
immigrants. These are not remarkable ideas, nor are
they contemptible. But like so many among the structuralist generation, Derrida is convinced that the only
way to extend the democratic values he himself holds
is to destroy the language in which the West has always conceived of them, in the mistaken belief that it
is language, not reality, that keeps our democracies
imperfect. Only by erasing the vocabulary of Western
political thought can we hope for a "repoliticization"
or a "new concept of politics." But once that point
is achieved, what we discover is that the democracy
we want cannot be described or defended; it can only
be treated as an article of irrational faith, a messianic
dream. That is the wistful conclusion of *Politics of
Friendship*:

> For democracy remains to come; this is its essence
> in so far as it remains: not only will it remain
> indefinitely perfectible, hence always insufficient
> and future, but, belonging to the time of the
> promise, it will always remain, in each of its
> future times, to come: even when there is democ-
> racy, it never exists.

Things have changed in Paris. The days when intellectuals turned to philosophers to get their political

bearings, and the public turned to intellectuals, are all
but over. The figure of the *philosophe engagé* promoted
by Sartre has been badly tarnished by the political
experiences of the past several decades, beginning with
the publication of Solzhenitsyn's books, then the Cam-
bodian horrors, the rise of Solidarity, and finally the
events of 1989. For structuralism in all its forms, it was
the disappointments of *le tiers monde* that did most to
call into question the philosophers' notion that cultures
are irreducibly different and men simply products of
those cultures. To their credit, some of the French intellectuals who became structuralists in the Fifties began
to see that the vocabulary they had once used to defend
colonial peoples against Western tyranny was now
being used to excuse crimes committed against those
peoples by homegrown, postcolonial tyrants.

Their abandonment of structuralism and deconstruction was not philosophically motivated, at least
at first; it was inspired by moral repugnance. But this
repugnance had the hygienic effect of reestablishing the
distinctions between, on the one hand, pure philosophy
and political philosophy and, on the other, committed
engagement. There is today a new French interest in
rigorous moral philosophy, epistemology, philosophy
of mind, and even cognitive science. The tradition of
political philosophy, ancient and modern, is also being
studied intensively for the first time in many years, and
there is some original theoretical work being done by
younger French political thinkers who are no longer
contemptuous of politicians or the state. This all could
change tomorrow, of course. But it is difficult to

imagine the French stepping into the structuralist river twice.

The persistent American fascination with Derrida and deconstruction has nothing to do with his current status in French philosophy, which is marginal at best. This raises a number of interesting questions about how and why his work has been received with open arms by American postmodernists, and what they think they are embracing. Derrida is often asked about his American success and always responds with the same joke: "*La déconstruction, c'est l'Amérique.*" By which he apparently means that America has something of the decentered, democratic swirl he tries to reproduce in his own thought. He may be onto something here, for if deconstruction is not America, it has certainly become an Americanism.

When continental Europeans think about questions of cultural difference and the Other, they are thinking about many deep and disturbing things in their own past: colonialism, nationalism, fascism, the Holocaust. What makes these historical events so difficult for them to grapple with is that there is no moderate liberal intellectual tradition in Europe that addresses them, or at least not a vigorous and continuous one. The Continental philosophical tradition makes it difficult to think about toleration, for example, except in the illiberal terms of Herder's Romantic theory of national spirit, the rigid French model of uniform republican citizenship, and now, most improbably, the idiosyncratic messianism of Jacques Derrida's deconstruction.

When Americans think about these issues of cultural difference they feel both pride and shame: pride in our capacity to absorb immigration and shame in the legacy of slavery that has kept black Americans a caste apart. The intellectual problem we face is not that of convincing ourselves that cultural variety can be good, or that differences should be respected, or that liberal political principles are basically sound. These we absorb fairly easily. The problem is in understanding why the American promise has only been imperfectly fulfilled, and how we should respond. About this we are clearly divided. But the fact that some political groups, such as those claiming to represent women and homosexuals, portray their moral enfranchisement as the logical extension of the social enfranchisement given to immigrants and promised, but never delivered, to American blacks, speaks volumes about the social consensus that exists in this country about how to think and argue about such questions.

In light of these contrasting experiences, it is a little easier to understand why the political reckoning structuralism faced in France during the Seventies and Eighties never took place in the United States. The souring of the postcolonial experiments in Africa and Asia and the collapse of Communist regimes nearby induced enormous self-doubt in Europe about the ideas that reigned in the postwar period. These same events have had no appreciable effect on American intellectual life, for the simple reason that they pose no challenge to our own self-understanding. When Americans read works in the structuralist tradition today, even in its most radicalized Heideggerian form in deconstruction, they find it difficult to imagine any moral and political implications they might have. People who believe it is possible to "get a new life" will not be overly concerned by the suggestion that all truth is socially constructed, or think that accepting it means relinquishing one's moral compass. That the antihumanism and politics of pure will latent in structuralism and deconstruction, not to mention the strange theological overtones that Derrida has recently added, are philosophically and practically incompatible with liberal principles sounds like an annoying prejudice.

No wonder a tour through the postmodernist section of any American bookshop is such a disconcerting experience. The most illiberal, anti-Enlightenment notions are put forward with a smile and the assurance that, followed out to their logical conclusion, they could only lead us into the democratic promised land, where all God's children will join hands in singing the national anthem. It is an uplifting vision and Americans believe in uplift. That so many of them seem to have found it in the dark and forbidding works of Jacques Derrida attests to the strength of Americans' self-confidence and their awesome capacity to think well of anyone and any idea. Not for nothing do the French still call us *les grands enfants*.

Afterword

THE LURE OF SYRACUSE

WHEN PLATO SET sail for Syracuse in 368 BC or so, he was, by his own report, of very mixed mind. He had visited that city once before when it was still ruled by the fearsome tyrant Dionysius the Elder, and the voluptuousness of Sicilian life did not appeal to him. How, he wondered, could young men learn to be moderate and just in a place where "happiness was held to consist in filling oneself full twice a day and never sleeping alone at night"? Such a city could never hope to escape the endless cycle of despotism and revolution.

So why return? As it happened, Plato did have a disciple in Sicily, whose soil was not as unforgiving as he had expected. A nobleman named Dion, who as a young man became devoted to Plato and the cause of philosophy, had just written him a letter reporting that Dionysius the Elder was dead and that his son, Dionysius the Younger, had taken command. Dion was both friend and brother-in-law to the younger Dionysius, and was convinced that the new ruler was open to philosophy and wished to be just. All he needed, in Dion's view, was to receive good instruction, which must come from Plato's own lips. He pleaded with his old teacher to visit, and Plato, overcoming serious misgivings, eventually set sail.

It is an old myth about Plato that he was the proponent of a mad scheme to institute the rule of "philosopher-kings" in Greek cities, and that his "Sicilian adventure" was a first step toward realizing his ambition. When Martin Heidegger returned to teaching in 1934 after his shameful tenure as Nazi rector of Freiburg University, a now forgotten colleague, meaning to heap more shame on his head, quipped, "Back from Syracuse?" As a bon mot this can hardly be bettered. But Plato's aims could not have been more different from Heidegger's. As Plato recounts in his *Seventh Letter*, he once dreamed of entering political life but was disheartened by the tyrannical rule of the Thirty in Athens (404–403 BC). He then renounced politics altogether when the democratic regime that succeeded the Thirty put to death his friend and teacher Socrates. He concluded, much as the character Socrates concludes in Plato's *Republic*, that once a political regime is corrupt there is little one can do to restore it to health "without friends and associates"—that is, without those who are both philosophical friends of justice and loyal friends of the city. Short of a miracle, in which philosophers would become kings or kings would turn to philosophy, the most that can be hoped for in politics is the establishment of a moderate government under the stable rule of law.

Dion, however, was a spirited man on the lookout for miracles. He convinced himself, and then tried to convince Plato, that Dionysius could be that rare thing, a philosophical ruler. Plato had his doubts; though he trusted Dion's character he also knew that "young men are often apt to fall prey to sudden and often inconsistent impulses." Yet he also reasoned—or perhaps rationalized to himself—that were he not to seize this rare opportunity and make the effort of turning a living tyrant toward justice he could be accused of cowardice and disloyalty to philosophy. And so he agreed to go.

But the outcome of this second visit was not happy. It was only too clear that Dionysius longed to acquire a patina of learning but lacked the discipline and commitment needed to submit to dialectical argument and bring his life into line with its conclusions. (Plato compares him to a man who wants to be in the sun but only manages to get himself sunburned.) Just as a doctor cannot cure a patient against his will, so it proved impossible to bring the stubborn Dionysius to philosophy and justice. In their conversations Plato and Dion even appealed to the young tyrant's political ambitions, telling him that as a philosopher he would learn how to give good laws to the cities he conquered, thus acquiring their friendship, which he could then exploit to extend his kingdom further. To no avail. Turning his ear to slanderous rumor, Dionysius instead grew to suspect Dion of harboring political ambitions of his own and summarily banished him from Syracuse. When Plato failed to bring about a reconciliation between the former friends, he decided to leave.

Yet six or seven years later he returned, again at Dion's behest. Although Dion was still in exile he had heard that Dionysius had returned to the study of philosophy, and reported this to Plato. At first Plato was unmoved, knowing that "philosophy often has this sort of effect on young men" and suspecting that Dionysius only wished to quell the gossip that Plato had rejected him as unworthy. But, following the same line of reasoning that led him to make the second trip, Plato decided to make a third, his last. What he discovered on arrival was an even haughtier man who already considered himself a philosopher and reportedly had written a book, something Plato the dialectician steadfastly refused to do. The cause was lost, yet Plato blamed no one but himself: "I had no more reason to be angry with Dionysius than with myself and with those who constrained me to come." Dion was not so sanguine. Three years after Plato's final departure he attacked Syracuse with mercenaries and liberated the city, expelling Dionysius, but was himself betrayed and murdered three years later. After a series of violent coups Dionysius eventually regained the throne, only to be deposed by the army of Corinth, Syracuse's mother city. Dionysius survived and returned to Corinth, where it is said he finished his days running a school, teaching his doctrines.

Dionysius is our contemporary. Over the last century he has assumed many names: Lenin and Stalin, Hitler and Mussolini, Mao and Ho, Castro and Trujillo, Amin and Bokassa, Saddam and Khomeini, Ceauşescu and Milosevic—one's pen runs dry. In the nineteenth century optimistic souls could believe that tyranny was a thing of the past. After all, Europe had entered the

modern age and everyone knew that complex modern
societies, attached to secular, democratic values, simply
could not be ruled by old-style despotic means. Modern
societies might still be authoritarian, their bureaucra-
cies cold and their workplaces cruel, but they could not
be tyrannies in the sense that Syracuse was. Modern-
ization would render the classical concept of tyranny
obsolete, and as nations outside Europe modernized
they, too, would enter the post-tyrannical future. We
now know how wrong this was. The harems and food-
tasters of ancient times are indeed gone but their places
have been taken by propaganda ministers and revolutionary guards, drug barons and Swiss bankers. The
tyrant has survived.

The problem of Dionysius is as old as creation. That
of his intellectual partisans is new. As continental
Europe gave birth to two great tyrannical systems in
the twentieth century, communism and fascism, it also
gave birth to a new social type, for which we need a
new name: the philotyrannical intellectual. A few major
thinkers of that period whose work is still meaningful
for us today dared to serve the modern Dionysius
openly in word and deed, and their cases are infamous:
Martin Heidegger and Carl Schmitt in Nazi Germany,
Georg Lukács in Hungary, perhaps a few others. A
great many joined Fascist and Communist parties on
both sides of the Iron Curtain, whether out of elective
affinities or professional ambition, without taking
great risks; a few played soldier for a time in the jungles
and deserts of the third world. A surprising number
were pilgrims to the new Syracuses being built in

Moscow, Berlin, Hanoi, and Havana. These were the political voyeurs who made carefully choreographed tours of the tyrant's domains with return tickets in hand, admiring the collective farms, the tractor factories, the sugarcane groves, the schools, but somehow never visiting the prisons.

Mainly, though, European intellectuals stayed at their desks, visiting Syracuse only in their imaginations, developing interesting, sometimes brilliant ideas to explain away the sufferings of peoples whose eyes they would never meet. Distinguished professors, gifted poets, and influential journalists summoned their talents to convince all who would listen that modern tyrants were liberators and that their unconscionable crimes were noble, when seen in the proper perspective. Whoever takes it upon himself to write an honest intellectual history of twentieth-century Europe will need a strong stomach.

But he will need something more. He will need to overcome his disgust long enough to ponder the roots of this strange and puzzling phenomenon. What is it about the human mind that made the intellectual defense of tyranny possible in the twentieth century? How did the Western tradition of political thought, which begins with Plato's critique of tyranny in the *Republic* and his unsuccessful trips to Syracuse, reach the point where it became respectable to argue that tyranny was good, even beautiful? Our historian will need to pose these larger questions, for he will find himself dealing with a general phenomenon, not isolated cases of extravagant behavior. The Heidegger case is only the most dramatic twentieth-century example of how philosophy, the love of wisdom, declined into philotyranny within living memory.

But where to begin? Our historian's first instinct may be to look to the history of ideas, on the assumption that intellectual philotyranny and modern tyrannical practices share common intellectual roots. He will find many learned investigations into the sources of modern political thought that share this assumption, and also share an approach, which is to divide the European intellectual tradition into rival tendencies and then brand one of them philotyrannical. A favorite target of such studies is the Enlightenment, which since the nineteenth century has been commonly portrayed as ripping the tangled roots of European society out of the loam of Christian religion and tradition, and encouraging cavalier experiments in reshaping society according to simple ideas of rational order.

According to this picture, the Enlightenment not only bred tyrannies, it was tyrannical in its very intellectual methods—absolutist, deterministic, inflexible, intolerant, unfeeling, arrogant, blind. This stream of adjectives is taken from the writings of Isaiah Berlin, who in a series of remarkably suggestive essays in intellectual history written in the postwar decades made the most sophisticated case thus far for blaming the theory and practice of modern tyranny on the *philosophes*. Berlin's main concern was the hostility to diversity and pluralism he discerned in a major current of the Western tradition that began with Plato and culminated intellectually in the Enlightenment, before bearing political fruit in twentieth-century totalitarianism. The cardinal assumptions of this stream of thought were that all moral and political questions have only one true answer, that those answers are accessible through reason, and that all such truths are necessarily compatible with one another. On these assumptions the gulags and death camps were built and defended. It was the Enlightenment that provided the ideal, in Berlin's words, "for which more human beings have, in our time, sacrificed themselves and others than, perhaps, for any other cause in human history."

This seems a convincing story. The problem with it, as our historian will undoubtedly see, is that it conflicts with another seemingly convincing story told by intellectual historians that reaches a rather different verdict about the intellectual responsibility for modern tyranny. This second story focuses on religious impulses rather than philosophical concepts, on the force of the irrational in human life, not on the pretensions of reason; it offers, one might say, intellectual history as Dostoevsky might have written it, not Rousseau. In the decades immediately following World War II much attention was given to religious irrationalism by Western historians who perceived a link between the theory and practice of modern tyranny and religious phenomena such as mysticism, messianism, chiliasm, kabbalism, and apocalyptic thought more generally. What they saw at work in the minds of revolutionaries and commissars was an old, irrational urge to hasten the coming of the Kingdom of God in a profane world. In The Pursuit of the Millennium (1957) Norman Cohn laid solid historical foundations for this approach. He demonstrated how significant were the outbursts of revolutionary millenarianism and mystical anarchism in Europe between the eleventh and sixteenth centuries and then drew parallels between the eschatological fantasies of that period and those of the twentieth century.

In his studies *The Origins of Totalitarian Democracy* (1952) and *Political Messianism* (1960), the Israeli historian Jacob Talmon brought this approach closer to the present by arguing, against Isaiah Berlin, that the most significant feature of European political thought in the eighteenth and nineteenth centuries was not its rationalism, which might have led it in a liberal direction, but rather the new religious fervor and messianic expectations with which modern democratic ideas became infused. In the frenzy of the French Revolution reason had ceased to be reasonable and democracy had become an ersatz religion for modern men bereft of traditional faith in the beyond. Only in these religious terms, Talmon thought, can we understand how the modern democratic ideal became a bloody tyrannical dream in the twentieth century.

Another apparently convincing story. But which of these two stories will our historian choose to tell? If he is like most historians that may well depend on which intellectual and political aspects of modern tyranny he feels deserve our attention. If he is trying to understand exclusively the brutality of Soviet "planning," the Nazis' chillingly efficient program to exterminate the Jews, the methodical self-destruction of Cambodia, the programs of ideological indoctrination, the paranoid webs of informers and secret police—if he wants to explain how these tyrannical practices were conceived and defended, he might be tempted to blame a heartless intellectual rationalism that crushed all in its path. If, on the other hand, he is struck by the role in modern tyranny played by the idolization of blood and soil, the hysterical obsession with racial categories, the glorification of revolutionary violence as a purifying force, the cults of personality, and the orgiastic mass rallies, he will be tempted to say that reason collapsed before irrational passions that had migrated from religion to politics. And if our historian is more ambitious still, and wants to explain both classes of phenomena? At that point he will have to abandon the history of ideas.

There is another way of investigating intellectual philotyranny, however. And that is to examine the social history of intellectuals in European political life, rather than the history of the ideas they held. Here, too, there are standard accounts that offer plausible explanations of philotyranny in the twentieth century. The most popular story is taken from the French experience. It begins with the Dreyfus Affair, which is portrayed by one and all as having expelled French intellectuals from the glades of *l'art pour l'art* and alerted them to their higher calling as moral watchmen over the modern state. The chapters that follow can be recited by every French schoolchild: the skirmishes between republican Dreyfusards and their Catholic-nationalist opponents; the splits over the Russian Revolution and the Popular Front after World War I; the intellectual and political compromises of Vichy; the dominance of Sartre's existential

Marxism after the war; the sharp divisions among intellectuals over Algeria; the revival of left-radicalism after May 1968; the *crise de conscience* after the publication of Solzhenitsyn's *Gulag Archipelago* in the 1970s, and the development of a liberal-republican consensus in the Mitterrand years.

The morals drawn from this story differ, however, depending on the political leanings of the narrator. As told by Jean-Paul Sartre this story became a heroic myth about the rise of the solitary "committed" intellectual who asserted his "singular universality" against the dominant ideology of bourgeois society and the tyrannical systems it had bred in Europe (fascism) and abroad (colonialism). In his influential *Plaidoyer pour les intellectuels*, texts of lectures given in 1965, Sartre portrayed the intellectual as a left-wing Jeanne d'Arc who stands for what is essentially human against the inhuman forces of economic and political "power," and also against those reactionary cultural forces, including traitorous fellow writers, whose work "objectively" supports the modern tyrant.

For his nemesis Raymond Aron, it was precisely this simple-minded opposition of "humanity" to "power" that demonstrated the incapacity of French intellectuals since the Dreyfus Affair to understand the real challenges of twentieth-century European politics. In Aron's view, it was no accident, indeed it was utterly predictable, that Sartre's romantic ideal of commitment would turn him into a heartless apologist for Stalinism in the decade after World War II. In *L'Opium des intellectuels* (1955) Aron retold the story of the rise of the modern intellectual but with a decidedly antimythical intent, demonstrating how incompetent and naive the intellectuals as a class had been when it came to serious political matters. In his view, the real responsibility of European intellectuals after the war was to bring whatever expertise they had to bear on liberal-democratic politics and to maintain a sense of moral proportion in judging the relative injustices of different political systems—in short, to be independent spectators with a modest sense of their roles as citizens and opinion-makers. Sartre and his followers accepted no such responsibilities.

Aron was right: in France it was the romantic, "committed" intellectuals who served the cause of tyranny in the twentieth century. But in Germany, which Aron knew uncommonly well, the picture was quite different. There the problem was, precisely, political disengagement. For a variety of reasons that historians of Germany discuss—the tradition of political decentralization, the lack of a cultural capital, the ideal of spiritual inwardness (*Innerlichkeit*), the autonomy of the university system, innate conservatism, and respect for military authority—Germany never developed an intellectual class along French lines, and consequently the issue of political commitment did not arise in the same way. East of the Rhine the assumption in the nineteenth and early twentieth centuries had been that professors were engaged in timeless *Wissenschaft* in the secluded university, that writers pursued private *Bildung* as they wrote their works, and that only journalists dared to write about politics, and they were untrustworthy.

This was a myth, of course, but a very attractive one in modern German culture. Nowhere is this more evident than in Thomas Mann's *Reflections of an Unpolitical Man* (1918), an intensely personal work that was also Mann's most ferociously political. Targeting his left-wing brother Heinrich, Mann tried to puncture the pretentions of the French *Zivilisationsliterat* with his childish attachment to democracy and popular enlightenment. Mann defended the tradition of German *Innerlichkeit* on aesthetic and political grounds. "German tradition," he wrote,

> is culture, soul, freedom, art and not civilization, society, voting rights, and literature. . . . Opposed to French *raison* and *esprit* is German *Innerlichkeit*, which guarantees that Germans never elevate social problems above moral ones, above inner experience.

Yet as he himself knew, and later came to regret, his principled "unpolitical" position carried great political meaning and served as a post hoc justification of German aims in World War I, encouraging the popular view that the Versailles peace was an act of cultural war. "This political spirit that is anti-German intellectually," he wrote, "is with logical necessity anti-German politically."

This was not the first time that an "unpolitical" German intellectual had made a disastrous political debut. At the creation of the Reich in 1871, at the outbreak of war in August 1914, and again in the

Walpurgisnacht of 1933, scores of Germany's leading professors and writers engaged themselves foolishly and ignorantly in politics, whether on the paradoxical grounds of defending the "unpolitical" German tradition, or out of a sudden naive embrace of politics, whose ways they did not begin to understand (Heidegger foremost among them). Most concluded that their forays into politics had been errors and returned quickly to their studies and laboratories.

The philosopher Jürgen Habermas, in a number of important postwar writings on the German political and cultural situation, has argued that this was exactly the wrong lesson to draw from these mistakes. By withdrawing from modern politics on principle, German writers and thinkers since the early nineteenth century had become accustomed to living in a mythical intellectual world governed by fantasies about Hellas or the Teutonic forests, fantasies that made Nazi tyranny appear to some of them as the beginning of spiritual and cultural regeneration. In Habermas's view, only by descending from the magic mountains of *Wissenschaft* and *Bildung* into the flatlands of democratic political discourse could German intellectuals have been inoculated against this tyrannical temptation, and had they done so they then might have helped to construct the open public sphere Germany needed—culturally and politically.

Habermas's argument seems convincing. But if he is right to blame German philotyranny on political disengagement, and Aron is right to blame blind political commitment in France, where does that leave our poor historian? Obviously neither explanation makes sense for twentieth-century Europe as a whole. It appears that just as neither "rationalism" nor "irrationalism" in the history of ideas can explain the theory and practice of modern tyranny, both "commitment" and "disengagement" in the social history of intellectuals fail to take us to the heart of the matter. All these attitudes and tendencies obviously had their part in European history, whether as proximate causes or effects, but none tells us why intellectual philotyranny develops at all. At this point our historian, if he is still with us, may begin to despair. Perhaps he will begin to wonder if the answer to his historical question is to be found in history or must be sought elsewhere. That would be a productive wonder, for it might encourage him to reexamine the old story of Plato, Dion, and Dionysius from another angle, looking for clues about the deeper forces that draw the mind to tyranny.

The most interesting fact about young Dionysius was that he was an intellectual. He may have been the first tyrant with such pretensions but he certainly was not the last. Today, in corners of left-leaning European bookshops, one can still find unwanted sets of Lenin's, Mao's, even Stalin's collected works, which were translated by propaganda bureaus in the Communist world and published by front organizations in the West. It may strike us as preposterous today that anyone would have felt the need to consult such works, or even to write them. But I doubt that Plato or Dion would have thought so. To judge by their actions in Syracuse, they understood that Dionysius's intellectual drive bore some important relation to his tyrannical political

ambitions—hence their hope that by working a transformation on the former they could indirectly moderate the latter. In the event, that turned out to be
impossible. Dionysius remained an immoderate glut-
ton for second- and third-hand ideas, which he regur-
gitated in written works that made a hash of Plato's
thought. But if Plato and Dion were mistaken in their
hopes, they were not necessarily wrong in their assumptions about the psychological force that draws certain
men to tyranny. It is the same force, Plato believed, that
draws other men to philosophy.

That force is love, eros. For Plato, to be human
is to be a striving creature, one who does not live
simply to meet his most basic needs but is somehow
driven to expand and sometimes elevate those needs,
which then become new objects of striving. Why do
humans "stretch" themselves in this way? For Plato
this is a deep psychological question, one to which
the characters in his dialogues offer many different
answers. Perhaps the loveliest is that given by Diotima
and reported by Socrates in the *Symposium*, that "all
men are pregnant in respect to both body and soul."
We are, or at least feel ourselves to be, incomplete creatures and cannot rest until some potential we sense
within is made actual, until we can "beget in the beautiful," as she puts it. This yearning, this eros, is to be
found within all our good and healthy desires, those of
the flesh and those of the soul; some people experience
mainly the former and satisfy themselves with their
bodies, while those who have desiring souls become
philosophers, poets, or concern themselves with "the

right ordering of cities and households"—that is, with politics in the highest sense. Wherever we see human activity for the good, Diotima tells Socrates, there we will find traces of eros.

But what of activity directed toward what is bad for us or others—drunkenness, say, or cruelty? Are these also driven by eros? In the *Phaedrus* Plato leads us to think so when he has Socrates introduce a famous image of the soul that pictures it as a team of two winged horses driven by a charioteer. One of these horses is said to be noble and is drawn toward what is eternal and true, while the other horse is something of a brute, lacking in control and unable to distinguish higher things from lower ones; he wants them all. If the base horse is stronger than the noble one, Socrates suggests, the soul will stay close to earth, but if the noble horse is stronger, or the charioteer can aid him, the soul rises closer to eternal truth. All souls—and therefore all human types—can be found somewhere on this celestial path, some closer to earth, others to the heavens, depending on how their erotic horses have traveled. Socrates describes nine such souls, the highest one being that of philosophers and poets, the lowest one belonging to the tyrant.

Love wants the good but it can also unwittingly serve the bad, Socrates explains. That is because love induces madness, a blissful kind of madness we find hard to control, whether we are in love with another human being or with an idea. But the highest happiness can only be had if such madness is indeed mastered and we remain in charge of our souls, even as eros draws us upward. Such self-mastery in the face of love is what the philosophical life aims to provide. As Plato paints it, the philosophical life is not one of Buddhist self-renunciation, it is a controlled erotic life that hopes to attain what love unconsciously seeks: eternal truth, justice, beauty, wisdom. Few are capable of such a life, and most of those who aren't will gratify their yearnings in predictable ways and lead middling lives. Others, though, become utter slaves to their drives and nothing will control them. These people Plato calls tyrants. In the *Republic* the character Socrates describes the tyrannical soul as one in which the madness of love—"love has from old been called a tyrant"—drives all moderation out and sets itself up as ruler, turning the soul itself into "a tyranny established by love." The philosopher also knows the madness of love, the love of wisdom, but he does not relinquish his soul to it; he remains in control, governing himself. The tyrannical man is the mirror image of the philosopher: he is not the ruler of his aspirations and desires, he is a man possessed by love madness, the slave of its aspirations and desires, rather than their ruler.

As the conversation in the *Republic* unfolds we learn that there is a connection between tyranny in the mind and tyranny in political life. Some tyrannical souls become rulers of cities and nations, and when they do entire peoples are subjugated by the rulers' erotic madness. But such tyrants are rare and their grip on power is weak. There is another, more common class of tyrannical souls that Socrates considers, those who enter public life not as rulers, but as teachers, orators, poets

—what today we would call intellectuals. These men can be dangerous, for they are "sunburned" by ideas. Like Dionysius, this kind of intellectual is passionate about the life of the mind, but unlike the philosopher he cannot master that passion; he dives headlong into political discussion, writing books, giving speeches, offering advice in a frenzy of activity that barely masks his incompetence and irresponsibility. Such men consider themselves to be independent minds, when the truth is that they are a herd driven by their inner demons and thirsty for the approval of a fickle public. Those who listen to such men, usually the young, may feel the stir of passion within; this feeling does them credit, for properly channeled it might bring honor to them and justice to their cities. But they are in need of an education in intellectual self-control if they are to turn that passion exclusively to good use.

Socrates understands this. These intellectuals, though, lack his humility and pedagogic care; their reputations depend on exciting passions, not channeling them. Socrates suggests that such intellectuals play an important role in driving democracies toward tyranny by whipping the minds of the young into a frenzy, until some of them, perhaps the most brilliant and courageous, take the step from thought to action and try to realize their tyrannical ambitions in politics. Then, gratified to see their own ideas take effect, these intellectuals become the tyrant's servile flatterers, composing "hymns to tyranny" once he is in power.

Socrates introduces the outrageous idea of philosopher-kings in the *Republic* to shake his interlocutors out of their complacency in thinking about this relationship between intellectuals and tyrants. The philosopher-king, were he to be born or bred, would abolish both. The philosopher-king is an "ideal," not in the modern sense of a legitimate object of thought demanding realization, but what Socrates calls a "dream" that serves to remind us how unlikely it is that the philosophical life and the demands of politics can ever be made to coincide. Reforming a tyranny may not be within our power, but the exercise of intellectual self-control always is. That is why the first responsibility of a philosopher who finds himself surrounded by political and intellectual corruption may be to withdraw. In the *Republic* Socrates likens the fate of a genuine philosopher in an imperfect city to "a human being who has fallen in with wild beasts and is neither willing to join them in doing injustice nor sufficient as one man to resist all the savage animals." Taking all this into the calculation, he keeps

> quiet and minds his own business—as a man in a storm, when dust and rain are blown about by the wind, stands aside under a little wall. Seeing others filled with lawlessness, he is content if somehow he himself can live his life here pure of injustice and unholy deeds, and take his leave from it graciously and cheerfully with fair hope.

Does this mean that Plato imagined the philosophical life as one of complete disengagement? Hardly. After delivering his speech about the philosopher in the windstorm, the character Socrates goes on to say that such a man does not lead the best life, for only in a good city "will he himself grow more and save the common things along with the private." And, as we know, the real-life Socrates was put to death for fighting tyranny, not in its explicitly political manifestations but at its psychological source in the human mind. The philosophical life represented by Socrates' own was, above all, an antityrannical life, the noblest one because it is supremely self-aware of its own tyrannical inclinations.

That self-awareness is what distinguishes the behavior of Plato and Dion in Syracuse from that of the philotyrannical intellectuals in twentieth-century Europe. Because Plato and Dion had followed Socrates' example and uprooted all tyranny from their own souls, they were able to understand the nature of Dionysius' rule and were justified in trying to free Syracuse from his tyranny. Both hoped that, as an intellectual, Dionysius might be turned to philosophy and be made to see the injustice of his actions and the foolishness of his writings. Both hoped to combat tyranny with the word, not the sword. They failed, and though afterward their paths separated, Plato returning to Athens and Dion descending to the battlefield, Plato defended both their actions. He recognized that, as a citizen of Syracuse who loved his homeland, Dion may have let his hopes mislead him about the chances of converting Dionysius and that he felt obliged to take up arms once their efforts failed. But Plato was confident that Dion did all this without letting the tyranny he combated enter his soul. There is no shame in failure or death in politics, so long as one remains free of that tyranny. Dionysius could never understand this simple principle. He survived but lived in dishonor, while Dion died a glorious death, loyal to truth and his city. "For to meet whatever fate sends in the attempt to reach the highest for oneself and one's country is altogether right and glorious," Plato concludes, in final judgment on his friend's life.

The lure of Syracuse is strong for any thinking man or woman, and that is as it should be. One need not accept Sartre's narcissistic myth of the intellectual as hero to see what Plato saw long ago: that there is some connection in the human mind between the yearning for truth and the desire to contribute to "the right ordering of cities and households." Yet precisely because Plato recognized this urge as an *urge*—as a drive that could become a reckless passion—he was alert to its destructive potential and concerned with harnessing it for a healthy intellectual and political life. One is tempted to say that it is this supreme self-awareness about how the mind handles ideas that distinguishes most fundamentally the philosopher in Plato's sense from so many modern intellectuals. And it is this same self-awareness that we would be wise to acquire in thinking about philotyranny in the twentieth century and learning from it.

It is difficult to think of a century in European history better designed than the last to excite the passions of the thinking mind and lead it to political disaster. The doctrines of communism and fascism, Marxism in all its baroque permutations, nationalism, *tiers-mondisme* —many inspired by a hatred of tyranny, all capable of inspiring hateful tyrants and blinding intellectuals to their crimes. It is possible to conceive of these tendencies as part of a grand historical narrative to which some external force, driving both events and their interpretations, can be ascribed. But no matter how much we reflect on such forces, we are still far from capturing the intimate struggles that European intellectuals had with them and the many ruses they employed to maintain their illusions.

As we read their works today and struggle to comprehend their actions, we need to get beyond our inner revulsion and confront the deeper *internal* forces at work in the philotyrannical mind—and, potentially, in our own. The ideologies of the twentieth century appealed to the vanity and raw ambition of certain intellectuals, but they also appealed, slyly and dishonestly, to the sense of justice and hatred of despotism that thinking itself seems to instill in us, and which, unmastered, can literally possess us. To those possessed, appeals to moderation and skepticism will appear cowardly and weak, which is why those rare European intellectuals who did invoke them—Aron was one—were subject to hateful attacks as traitors to their calling. Such men may not have been philosophers in the classical sense but they did display the same intellectual and political sang-froid that Plato thought distinguished the genuine philosopher from the irresponsible intellectual.

Hard cases make bad law, so the judges have decreed. Perhaps, then, we should turn a blind eye to the political mistakes of European intellectuals and try to understand them in light of the extreme circumstances of the twentieth century and hope for calmer days ahead. Our historian may feel this temptation acutely. But he would be mistaken to give in to it. Tyranny is not dead, not in politics and certainly not in our souls. The age of the master ideologies may be over, but so long as men and women think about politics—so long as there are thinking men and women at all—the temptation will be there to succumb to the allure of an idea, to allow passion to blind us to its tyrannical potential, and to abdicate our first responsibility, which is to master the tyrant within.

The events of the last century merely provided the occasion for extraordinary displays of intellectual philo-tyranny whose sources will not disappear in less extreme political circumstances, for they are part of the makeup of our souls. If our historian really wants to understand the *trahison des clercs*, that is where he, too, must look: within.

ACKNOWLEDGMENTS

Early versions of Chapters I, II, III, VI, and the Afterword appeared originally in *The New York Review of Books*. Early versions of Chapters IV and V appeared originally in *The Times Literary Supplement*. Permission to reprint is gratefully acknowledged.

3 5282 00553 6886